Orchid

grower's companion

Orchid
grower's companion

Cultivation, Propagation, and Varieties

David P. Banks

Timber Press
Portland, Oregon

A QUINTET BOOK

Published in 2005 by
Timber Press, Inc.
The Haseltine Building
133 S.W. Second Avenue, Suite 450
Portland, Oregon 97204-3527, U.S.A.

www.timberpress.com

ISBN 0-88192-711-2

A catalog record for this book is available from the Library of Congress

This book was designed and produced by
Quintet Publishing Limited, London

Project editor Catherine Osborne
Art director Roland Codd
Designer Pritty Ramjee
Principal photographer David P. Banks
Step-by-step photography Jeremy Thomas

Creative director Richard Dewing
Associate publisher Laura Price
Publisher Oliver Salzmann

Manufactured by Universal Graphics Pte Ltd, Singapore
Printed by SNP Leefung Printers Limited, China

Dedication
*This book is dedicated, with much love and gratitude, to my wife
Louanne, and my parents – Graeme and Lynette Banks.*

Author Acknowledgements
I wish to thank the following people for encouragement,
support, advice and in many cases, plants from their private
collections; David Butler, Anna Chai, Ray Clement, Jim
Cootes, Andy Easton, Ian & Robin Flood, Howard Gunn,
Michael Harrison, Tom Perlite, Andy Phillips, John Roberts,
Terry Root, Norm Shipway, Darryl Smedley, Gerardus Staal,
Gowan Stewart, David Titmuss, Marni Turkel and Dieter
Weise. I am also most appreciative of the countless orchid
enthusiasts, throughout the world (including the above-
mentioned), that have allowed me to photograph their
choice orchids.

Most importantly, I would like to particularly thank my
parents, Lynette and Graeme Banks, who have always
encouraged me, as well as my wife Louanne and daughter
Rebekah for ongoing love and support.

David P. Banks
Hills District Orchids
Seven Hills, NSW, Australia.
Email: dpbanks@ozemail.com.au
August 2004

Further Acknowledgements
The publisher would like to thank Jim Durrant and the staff
at McBeans Orchids for all their help on the photo shoot for
most of the propagation sequences used within this title.

CONTENTS

INTRODUCTION

Orchids are the monarchs of the plant kingdom, arguably being the largest family of flowering plants. They are certainly the most diverse, with an array of fascinating and gorgeous blooms. Mention orchids and exotic, rare, expensive, beautiful, and colorful are the words that immediately spring to mind. Many people are under the misconception that orchids are difficult to grow and that you must have elaborate greenhouses to cultivate a selection of plants. However this is simply not the case, with many types as easy to maintain in the home as other ornamental houseplants.

This book is the ideal starting place for a journey into the colorful and flamboyant world of orchids and their successful cultivation. There are chapters on what defines an orchid, their history in cultivation and geographical distribution, as well as the issues affecting their conservation in the wild, and on judging and exhibiting show plants. A major portion of the book comprises a directory of orchids, presenting a photographic display of over 400 quality orchid species and hybrids recommended for the home gardener. Coupled with the directory, there's a practical chapter providing the most up-to-date cultivation and propagation advice. Here, you will find all the information you need to grow orchids to their maximum potential in your own home and garden.

Most orchids are easy to grow as long as their housing, temperature, and moisture needs are met. The best plant and orchid growers are those who are attentive, notice slight differences in the health of their plants, and respond accordingly. This means you need to be observant, and a little bit of a detective. The excellent information in the Cultivation and Care chapter comes from first-hand expert experience, providing professional advice and tips on caring for your orchid.

It is estimated that there are over 30,000 different orchid species on our planet and new species are still being discovered and recorded. On top of this, there are well over 100,000 registered hybrid strains, which have been artificially propagated. Many of these hybrids are important commercial plants; being used as cut flowers and pot plants to satisfy a strong international demand. Few orchids have "common" names and many are simply referred to by their "botanical" or generic name. This has happened with many other groups of plants, where people use botanical names as common names—often without knowing it. Such tongue-twisting examples include *Agapanthus, Chrysanthemum, Jacaranda,* and *Rhododendron,* names derived from both Latin and Greek. Latin is used for scientific terms to enable a universal system for communication, and avoid the difficulty of common names that may refer to completely different plants, or perhaps a "local" name in one area which may not be known in another.

Growing orchids is an enjoyable, rewarding, and sometimes challenging pastime. You are forever learning about them, as new species are still being found, "lost" plants are being rediscovered, and new hybrids are flowering for the first time. You will see from the photographs in this work that orchids come in a vast array of shapes, sizes, and colors. They are highly specialized plants, which will continue to captivate future generations with their unique beauty. Most of all, orchids are exciting and deeply gratifying to grow. And be warned—orchid growing may become an addiction. I hope the guidance and advice you find here will lead to a life-long indulgence.

Part One

THE NATURE
OF ORCHIDS

The unique beauty of orchids has made them the most exotic and desirable flower in the plant kingdom. They are the most advanced and complex of all plants, with the greatest variation in plant form and function. Nevertheless they are instantly recognizable whether they are the commonest hybrid in a florist shop or the latest and rarest miniature species from the slopes of Mount Kinabalu.

The word "orchid" is a derivation from the Greek word *orchis*, meaning testis, which refers to the pair of testiculate underground tubers that are frequently seen in Mediterranean terrestrial orchids such as *Orchis*, *Ophrys,* and *Dactylorhiza*. In Greek and Asian culture, the tubers were crushed into a paste and frequently used to treat various ailments and added to drinks for their alleged aphrodisiac qualities. Even today, some orchids are used in traditional Chinese medicine.

PLANT STRUCTURE

RIGHT *Vandas are important plants for cut flower production throughout Southeast Asia. This is* Vanda Gordon Dillon *'Gowan.'*

There are two main growth structures in orchids, monopodial and sympodial. Sympodial orchids, such as *Bulbophyllum, Cattleya, Dendrobium,* and *Oncidium,* have a main stem or pseudobulb that is produced annually but matures at the end of each growing season, often culminating with flowering. Next season, a new pseudobulb grows from the base of last season's growth. These pseudobulbs, which hold water and nutrients, are produced along a connecting stem structure known as a rhizome.

Monopodial orchids such as *Angraecum, Phalaenopsis, Sarcochilus,* and *Vanda* do not have a pseudobulb but have a main stem that is in constant growth. They produce flower spikes, correctly termed inflorescences, from or opposite the leaf axil.

Most orchids are epiphytes. These grow on trees for support and light, avoiding the darkness of the forest floor. They also receive ample air circulation and their root systems are always well drained. They are neither parasitic, as they do not take food from the tree, nor are they symbiotic, as the host receives no benefit at all from this one-sided relationship. Instead the tree merely acts as a support or substrate, providing perfect conditions for the orchid to grow and thrive.

Some species grow exclusively on rocks and these are known as lithophytes. Species that grow in the ground are referred to as terrestrials. Most of the tropical terrestrial orchid species, such as *Phaius* and *Neobenthamia,* are evergreen as opposed to the deciduous terrestrials (including *Corybas, Cypripedium,* and *Pterostylis*), which are more prevalent in temperate climates. After flowering, these deciduous orchids die down to storage organs, known as tubers, and have a similar life cycle to bulbs. Their growth cycle starts once the harsher weather has passed.

ABOVE
Phalaenopsis *orchids are ideal flowering plants for cultivation in the home. The long-lasting blooms and compact plants ensure their popularity.*

A small percentage of all orchids are saprophytes. These live off dead or decaying matter and have no green parts. There are even two unusual Australian orchid species, *Rhizanthella gardneri* and *Rhizanthella slateri,* that grow and flower completely underground.

Orchid plants vary in size from true miniatures, such as the epiphytic Australian species *Bulbophyllum minutissimum* and *Bulbophyllum globuliforme* (with pseudobulbs about ⅛ inch [2 to 3 mm] in diameter and needle-like leaves about ¹⁄₁₀ inch [1 to 2 mm] long), to free-standing orchids such as the recently described *Sobralia* species from South America (with cane-like stems up to 25 feet [8 m] tall). Some orchids, such as *Vanilla,* grow as vines, and mature plants can reach to over 100 feet (30 m) long.

ABOVE Laelia anceps *and an* Epidendrum *species, clinging to trees in the wild for support and sunlight.*

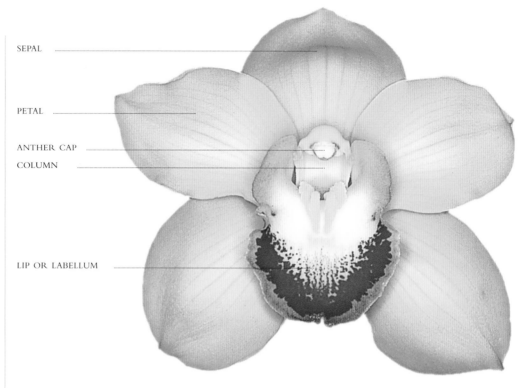

SEPAL

PETAL

ANTHER CAP
COLUMN

LIP OR LABELLUM

The basic flower structure of an orchid

Flower Structure

Orchids are monocots, that is, they belong to the same group as lilies and as a result have their floral parts arranged in threes or multiples of three: three petals, three sepals. The flowers of orchids are often bilaterally symmetrical (zygomorphic), that is the left-hand side is a mirror image of the right-hand side. The third petal, known as the lip or labellum, is almost always highly modified and often quite different in size, shape, and color from the other petals and sepal. The lip is usually lower-most and acts as a landing platform, attractant, or guide to pollinators. However, the main characteristic of an orchid is the fusion of the stamens (male) and pistil (female) sexual parts to form a single structure called the column. Often the single anther (male) lies at or near the apex of the column and contains the pollen. Unlike most plants, orchid pollen is borne in discrete masses called pollinia containing thousands of pollen grains. Depending on the species, pollinia can number two, four, or eight.

Orchid Seeds

Orchid seeds are minute and dust-like with a single fruit or capsule that matures behind the spent flower. Depending on the species, they have the potential to produce over a million seeds. However, orchid seeds have little food storage capacity and rely on a specific type of fungus for their germination and development. The mortality rate in the

RIGHT
A Dendrobium
macrophyllum *seed capsule. Today orchid seeds are germinated in laboratories using a synthetic agar solution.*

wild is enormous. Today, orchid seeds are germinated in laboratories using a synthetic agar solution. This has enabled large quantities of both species and hybrids to be produced in what is essentially a sterile environment. Depending on the genus, orchids can take anything between 12 months to 12 years from germination to flowering. On average, most orchids flower around four years from germination—they start out in life as green "blobs" known as protocorms.

It surprises many that *Vanilla* or *Vanilla planifolia* is actually an orchid. This plant grows like a vine and is suited to moist, tropical climates. Its seed capsules are used for culinary flavoring even though synthetic substitutes are widely available. The flowers last only a day and need to be hand-pollinated to ensure that the "vanilla pods" will form.

Orchid Roots

Orchid roots serve a number of purposes. Rock and tree dwellers use their roots to attach firmly to their host to avoid being dislodged during strong winds or storms, or being taken away by birds or animals. Epiphytic orchid roots are generally white in color and have a green growing tip. Behind the root tip, the root is covered by an envelope of dead empty cells called a velamen. The velamen acts like a sponge and absorbs water very quickly. They can be kept turgid by being exposed to mists and fog.

Some orchids, such as a number of *Cymbidium, Catasetum,* and *Dendrobium* species, will also produce a thicket of upright litter-collecting roots that point straight up in the air. As these orchids can grow into sizable clumps in the wild, they often build up quite a garden of rotting vegetation that has fallen from above.

The roots of terrestrial orchids primarily secure the plant but also take up food and water, with most deciduous genera (such as *Pterostylis* and *Pleione*) losing their entire root system when the plant enters

dormancy. Once they reshoot, a new crop of roots is quickly produced by the plant which assist its growth.

The dried pseudobulbs of some of the larger growing *Dendrobium* species from New Guinea have been used in handicrafts, whereas Australian Aborigines have been known to roast the tubers of different species of orchids and the pseudobulbs of the native *Cymbidium* species for food.

ABOVE Vanilla planifolia *is the vine-like species from which vanilla extract is produced, after processing of the long, dried seed capsule.*

POLLINATION

The infinite variation in the shape of orchid flowers has evolved to attract pollinators and to make them effective dispersers of pollen. Many creatures pollinate orchids, and the flowers use their form, color, and often fragrance to attract these pollinators.

The various types of slipper orchid—*Cypripedium, Paphiopedilum,* and *Phragmipedium*—have a modified pouch-like labellum with slippery inner sides. The insects that fall into the labellum can only exit the flower by crawling out of the narrow gap between the top of the lip and the sticky pollen masses. This process is repeated when the insect visits another flower, only this time it deposits its pollen load onto the stigmatic surface of the slipper orchid's bloom.

Numerous orchid flowers actually mimic insects (both in appearance and scent) and rely on the insects for what is called pseudo-copulation. Here male insects, generally bees and wasps, do all the work. In a fascinating example of co-evolution, the orchid blooms emit the same scent as the female, and raised calli or ridges on parts of the labellum mimic the potential mate. It is only the male wasp that has wings and can fly in search of his potential mating partner. The female wasps are wingless and literally crawl up blades of grass, emit their pheromones or sexual fragrance, and wait for a male to literally pick them up and mate with them "on the wing." In the case of many of the Australian terrestrial orchids, such as *Caladenia, Chiloglottis,* and *Cryptostylis,* the orchids bloom only a month or so before the female wasps emerge. The male wasps are already searching for a potential mate and are attracted to the sight and smell of the orchid flower. Mistaking the orchid for the female insect, the wasp attempts to mate with the flower. In doing so, pollen is

BELOW LEFT
Wild orchid Ophrys scolopax *which mimics a bee. The labellum imitates the shape, color, and smell of the female long-horned bee* Eucera longicornis.

BELOW RIGHT
Paphiopedilum hangianum*'s labellum is a modified pouch, designed purely to aid pollination. It is native to northern Vietnam.*

RIGHT *A long-horned bee* Eucera longicornis *pollinating an* Ophrys scolopax *orchid. Male bees are sexually attracted to the flower and attempt to mate with it. In the process of male bee movements, the head of* Eucera *brushes against the pollen bearing "pollinaria" of the flower and these are released onto the bee's head. The bee carries this yellow pollen structure to another orchid plant and acts as a pollinator.*

deposited on the end of their bodies. When they attempt the same with another flower of the same species, pollination takes place. It is amazing that the size of the orchid blooms and their precise positioning allow this to take place. Often, only a particular species of insect will visit a particular species of orchid. In the case of the European bee orchids, *Ophrys*, not only do the orchid flowers look like female bees but they also smell and feel like the female bee (the hairs on the orchid are exactly the same structure to those on the bee)!

Other orchids, such as the Australian donkey orchids, *Diuris*, deceive bees by looking like flowers that offer a reward. In New Guinea there are many *Dendrobium* species, such as *Dendrobium lawesii*, which have brightly colored and long-lasting tubular blooms that actually mimic the epiphytic *Rhododendron* species growing in the same forests. Yet, the pollinator gets no reward in this one-sided exercise because, unlike the *Rhododendron*, the orchid does not produce nectar.

There are others with dark maroon flowers that smell like rotten flesh, such as

Bulbophyllum fletcherianum from New Guinea and related *Bulbophyllum* species, that attract flies and carrion beetles. The *Stanhopea* and *Coryanthes* species from South America are in bloom for only a few days, yet emit a very strong fragrance when in bloom, to attract a specific bee to perform the pollination duties.

Color

Orchids come in every color, including bright blues, glorious reds, even blooms that appear black, and they all have a meaning if we can read the signs. Generally, the yellow flowers attract the attention of bees, while green and white flowers are usually pollinated in the evening by moths. Orange and red tubular flowers, such as the genus *Masdevallia,* are often pollinated by nectar-seeking hummingbirds. These and other species are so effective in deceiving the birds that they actually have no nectar. Blooms come in a range of glorious colors with intricate veined or spotted patterns.

RIGHT *The fragrant nighttime smell of* Angraecum Veitchii *attracts nocturnal moths who pollinate the flower when feeding on its nectar-filled spur.*

BELOW *The large size and bright colors of the* Oncidium Mendenhall 'Green Valley' *help to attract potential pollinators, most often bees, wasps, and even butterflies.*

Scent

Because several popular corsage orchids (like the large hybrid cymbidiums) lack a strong scent, orchids often have the reputation of being scentless. However nothing could be further from the truth, and the overwhelming perfume of the glossy purple *Cattleya* is just one example of the many highly scented orchids that are out there.

Many of the white- and green-flowered angraecoid orchids (*Angraecum, Aerangis,* and relatives) from Madagascar and Africa have blooms that are fragrant only in the evening. Their scent attracts nocturnal moths, who play an active role in their pollination. The orchids have a nectar-filled spur at the base of the lip or labellum, which varies in length between the different species. The nectar supply is at the end of this spur, so the pollinating moth must have a tongue or proboscis long enough to claim the reward. As it feeds on the nectar, the moth ends up with pollen on its head or proboscis, which is later deposited onto another flower thus completing the pollination process.

When seeing *Angraecum sesquipedale* for the first time, the naturalist Charles Darwin suggested that a massive moth must pollinate this orchid's large blooms, which measured over 8 inches (20 cm) across, with a spur up to 13 inches (33 cm) long. At the time, he was ridiculed for this suggestion because there was no moth on record that had such a long tongue. Sadly, Darwin did not live to learn that years later a massive moth was discovered, the Madagascan hawk moth, that had a proboscis measuring over 1 foot (30 cm), long enough to reach the nectar at the end of *Angraecum sesquipedale*'s spur. It was given the scientific name *Xanthopan morgani praedicta,* the last epithet in recognition of its theorized existence.

The genus *Brassavola* and related *Rhyncholaelia* from Central and South America also have scented blooms that rely on moths for pollination. *Brassavola nodosa* is called the "lady of the night" because of the sweet pleasant fragrance it omits after sunset.

UNDERSTANDING ORCHID NAMES

The term "species orchid" relates to the plants as they occur naturally in the wild. Each species has a generic name, (or first term), for example *Laelia*, plus a specific epithet, (or second term), for example *anceps*. The two terms combine to form the specific name of the species: *Laelia anceps*.

When written they are in *italics* or underlined. The generic name always begins with a capital letter but the specific epithet is written with a small letter first—even when it is derived from a personal name.

A varietal epithet (third term) is given to a distinctive race or population within a species. It is preceded by the abbreviation var. (for variety), subsp. (for subspecies), or f. (for forma) [Generally used for albinistic color variants] which is in roman letters. The varietal epithet is in *italics*, or underlined without a capital.

A special clone of a species may be given a cultivar epithet (third or fourth term). This is in roman, with a capital, and has single quotes. Inexplicably, many experienced growers still confuse cultivars with varieties.

BELOW Cattleya *(generic name/first term)* bicolor *(specific epithet/second term)* 'Golden Gate' *(the name of the special clone of the species/third term).*

Natural Hybrids

Most "wild" orchids are pure species, without the genetic infusion of other different species. Natural hybrids are rare and the ones that do exist are usually a combination of two related species. These often occur as single plants, but sometimes they can form hybrid swarms. Natural hybrids should be written in *italics* with a capital multiplication symbol (in roman) between the generic name and the specific epithet. For example, *Cattleya × venosa*. This is the naturally occurring hybrid between the species *Cattleya forbesii* and *Cattleya harrisoniana*.

Artificial Hybrids

These are hybrids deliberately created by man to exploit desirable horticultural traits in the orchid blooms. It may be for characters such as color, size, shape, floriferousness, or perfume.

The generic name (first term) begins with a capital letter and is in *italics* (preferred) or underlined. The second term is the name of a registered manmade hybrid combination, known as a "grex epithet." It is not Latinized or underlined. It is printed in roman letters and the initial letter is a capital.

RIGHT *Two examples
of the hybrid*
Paphiopedilum
*Maudiae (*callosum ×
lawrencianum)*, one the
albino form, the other
the normal colored form.*

RIGHT
Paphiopedilum
Enchantress.

FAR RIGHT
Cymbidium *Australian
Midnight 'Tinonee' is a
special clone of a hybrid
and is distinguised by a
cultivar epithet. These
are only given to
superior clones of
horticultural merit.*

A special clone of a hybrid may be distinguished by a cultivar epithet. These are generally only given to superior clones of horticultural merit. It is in roman letters, has a capital, and is in single quotes. Remember there are no "varieties" in hybrid orchids, only cultivars.

In orchids, the same grex or hybrid group applies to all the progeny raised from any "mating" of two parent plants that bear the *same pair* of specific names and/or grex names. For example, if any plant of the grex *Dendrobium* Hilda Poxon is crossed with any plant of the species *Dendrobium kingianum*, the resulting progeny will all bear the grex name *Dendrobium* Telekon. All official orchid hybrids are registered with the Royal Horticultural Society, London. These new names appear in periodicals such as *The Orchid Review* (UK), *Orchids* (USA), and in the Australian publications *The Australian Orchid Review*, *Orchids Australia,* and *The Orchadian* (for Australian native orchid hybrids only). These hybrids later appear (every five years) in updated volumes of *Sander's List of Orchid Hybrids*, which is also now available on CD-ROM.

EXAMPLES

Cymbidium Australian Midnight 'Tinonee'
<u>Cymbidium</u> Australian Midnight 'Tinonee'

Botanical Communication

Plants are given scientific or botanical names to enable global communication on a specific taxon, which is the collective name for a particular distinct species, subspecies, or variety. Common names do not work, as they may be applied to many (often unrelated) plants. For example, there are well over a dozen different orchids that are known as "spider orchids."

According to the International Code of Botanical Nomenclature, the earliest valid description of a species has priority. This principle is fairly clear-cut and easily applied but it can be frustrating, particularly when the name of the plant has become entrenched in botanical and horticultural circles. For example, the well-known

Philippine species *Dendrobium gonzalesii* (named by Quisumbing in 1938) relates to the same species that Reichenbach described as *Dendrobium ceraula* 62 years previously in 1876. Therefore the name *Dendrobium ceraula* takes priority and *Dendrobium gonzalesii* becomes a synonym.

There is also the ongoing lumpers versus splitters debate. Lumpers are taxonomists or scientists who prefer to refer to similar species of orchids under the one name, whereas splitters don't allow for a wide variation in the characters of a particular species and prefer to redefine "different" or "unusual" populations of such plants as different species, not allowing for a wide variation within a given taxon. In the Australian dendrobiums, arguably the most controversial example is *Dendrobium speciosum.* The lumpers prefer to look at it as a variable species, while the splitters have embraced the decision to regard it as a species complex and reclassify it into five closely related species. It also happens at a higher level with sections, or closely related species within a genus, removed into their own genera. We have already started to see this with the segregation of *Dendrobium* into a number of splinter genera, such as *Dockrillia* and *Grastidium*. This is also occurring with other, diverse, large genera such as *Bulbophyllum, Epidendrum, Eria, Liparis, Maxillaria, Odontoglossum, Oncidium, Pleurothallis, Pterostylis,* and *Vanda*. Even though these studies are supported by DNA analysis, they are still open to discussion and interpretation. The classification of orchids is an artificial process and naming them gives us a common point of reference which aids global communication.

ABOVE Dendrobium speciosum. *There is an ongoing debate about this orchid as to whether it is a variable species or a species complex.*

THE HISTORY OF ORCHID CULTIVATION

Orchids have historically been linked to the adventurous and the wealthy. While it is documented that the Chinese were cultivating some of their fragrant *Cymbidium* species as early as 500 BC and the Japanese nurtured specimens of the endemic *Neofinetia falcata*, it was not until the late eighteenth century and early nineteenth century that orchid growing became widely popular.

ABOVE Neofinetia falcata *Anami Island Type, one of the first specimens nurtured by the Japanese.*

This coincided with the British Empire's spread throughout the world in the late eighteenth century to both colonize new lands as well as bring back trophies of plants and animals found during exploration. The length of the ocean voyages meant the merchant ships often could only bring back dried or herbarium specimens, as the plants simply could not survive the long journeys.

In the late 1800s, the possession of epiphytic orchids became the ultimate status symbol among British gardening aristocrats. These tree-growing orchids were not indigenous to Europe and were therefore extremely rare. To accommodate these exotic tropical plants, British aristocrats built enormous glasshouses or "stovehouses."

Subsequent voyages, sponsored by wealthy nurserymen, brought back vast quantities of orchids and other horticulturally desirable plants including aroids, palms, ferns, cycads, *Nepenthes* pitcher plants, and other botanical oddities. Only a small percentage survived these trips, with most of the shipments perishing en route, either rotting, desiccating, or being eaten by the rats on board the ships.

Victorian Status Symbols

Orchid possession became a status symbol, with vast amounts of money offered and spent on the latest botanical introductions. Orchid nurseries were established and there was intense competition between them to secure the more spectacular species. Some of the larger orchid nurseries of the day were run by family concerns, and the names Loddiges, Williams, Bull, Veitch, and Sander became prominent in the early history of European orchid growing, with many new species and varieties named after them. Arguably, the most successful and distinguished of these was Frederick Sander —known as the Orchid King.

Sander developed one, if not *the*, largest collection of orchids and tropical plants of the day, with over 60 fully stocked glasshouses. He boasted that he had plant collectors "all around the world"— including Borneo, the Philippines, and New Guinea. His plant collectors had to contend with tropical diseases, venomous snakes, and often unfriendly natives, as well as the dangers of sea travel—both from the unpredictable weather and from the threat of pirates. Some never made the safe return voyage. When the ships made their way back home, Sander would evaluate the shipment and often send them back

LEFT *Orchid collectors traveled far and wide for the most exotic orchids, some even died in their quest for unknown and mythical species such as the blue slipper orchid.*

BELOW *Booth's Sand Lady is a primary hybrid with* Paphiopedilum sanderianum *as one of the parents.*

immediately if the more spectacular species had perished.

Transportation subsequently improved, and this significantly reduced the numbers of plants that were damaged at sea. Many delicate plants were placed in Wardian Cases for transport, which resembled large glass fish tanks. This regular importation of the very latest in tropical orchids had a devastating impact on populations in the wild. There are a majority of orchid species that are exceedingly rare in the wild to this day because of the indiscriminate over-collecting during that period.

Prestige Plants

There was little love lost between the competing orchid nurseries, with many of them striving for the next "prestige plant" to be added to their collections and catalogs. The locations of specific plants would be a closely guarded secret, and obscure localities were passed off in an attempt to put rival collectors off the scent of new finds. Some even encouraged rivals into thick forested territories known to be the homes of

headhunters! This happened when rivals were seeking the regal slipper orchid, *Paphiopedilum rothschildianum,* in New Guinea (now known to be endemic to Mount Kinabalu in Sabah, Borneo). It never actually existed in New Guinea, and this lie was perpetuated when Linden's nursery sold plants under the unpublished name of *Cypripedium neo-guineense.*

While it was the collectors who actually brought many of the new species to the Western world, it was the wealthy nurserymen, botanists, and plant collectors that were immortalized when "new" species were named in their honor.

Sander ensured that some of the finest species were named after his family, including *Paphiopedilum sanderianum, Dendrobium sanderae, Maxillaria sanderiana,* and *Vanda sanderiana* (which is sometimes classified as *Euanthe sanderiana*).

The Sander orchid dynasty lasted for over a century and their name is perpetuated in the ongoing list of registered orchid hybrids, known as *Sander's List of Orchid Hybrids.*

Spectacular Introductions

The name Veitch is synonymous with orchids. James Veitch founded a nursery that was expanded to its full potential by his son, Harry Veitch. Harry, who was later knighted for his services to the horticultural industry, staged the Great Horticultural Exhibit of 1866. In later years, this evolved into the Chelsea Flower Show. While primarily interested in species plants, many groundbreaking primary hybrids were developed at Veitch's nursery. Some of these are still in cultivation today, including *Angraecum* Veitchii (*sesquipedale* × *eburneum*), *Epiphronitis* Veitchii (*Epidendrum radicans* × *Sophronitis coccinea*), and *Thunia* Veitchiana (*marshalliana* × *bensonii*).

When many of these exotic orchids were introduced to the stovehouses for the first time few of them flourished. Many of them were from countries near the equator, and nursery owners therefore assumed that they needed very hot and humid conditions. In reality, this suited only a handful of species from the tropical lowlands, and the montane species from the cooler mountains quickly perished. The English stovehouses were literally cooking the plants in the stifling heat. Collectors were sent to gather more information about the conditions in which the orchids were growing and as a result, head gardeners learned that many of the orchids required cooler temperatures, in particular a significant drop in the evening, with plenty of fresh air circulating around the plants. A number of glasshouses were modified to house specific genera and these were kept at different temperature ranges with varying amounts of shade.

In the late 1800s, most of the orchids supplied to enthusiasts were either species from wild collected stock or divisions taken from existing plants in cultivation. Orchid seed proved very difficult to germinate, with most success achieved when seed was sown on the tops of established plants that had healthy, and slightly exposed, root systems. Many of the first hybrids were also grown from these humble beginnings. The seeds required a mycorrhizal fungus, present in the roots of mature plants, to assist germination. Despite the hundreds or thousands of viable seeds sown, the results were disappointing, with only a few, if any, germinating and reaching maturity in the years ahead.

It was not until 1917 that the American, Lewis Knudson, developed a technique to germinate orchid seeds in sterile glass flasks, on an artificial culture medium, composed of agar and plant nutrients. This method, with minor variations, is used today for the germination of most orchid genera. It enabled the plants to be mass-produced, and meant that nurseries could cater to their customers needs on a supply-and-demand basis. Plants that were once very rare and expensive were readily available at affordable prices and it was this that opened up orchid growing to a wider audience.

Monographs and Color Plates

Successful nurserymen published lavish catalogs of the many and varied plants they were cultivating, including many volumes devoted to orchids. James Veitch and Sons published *A Manual of Orchidaceous Plants* between 1887–1894. These significant works provided habitat information and cultivation tips that are still pertinent today. Other lavish Victorian and Edwardian color-plate books were released in limited editions, showcasing some of the more spectacular introductions as well as some of the early manmade hybrids. The Royal Horticultural Society and Kew Gardens devoted a lot of their energy to promoting the hobby of orchid cultivation, and in 1893 launched its periodical, *The Orchid Review*. This is currently issued bimonthly, with over 1,250 issues distributed worldwide.

ABOVE Epiphronitis Veitchii, *one of the many groundbreaking primary hybrids developed at James Veitch's nursery.*

ABOVE *Elaborate and beautiful illustrations of orchids, like the two above, appeared in lavish catalogs published by successful nurserymen.*

ORCHID SOCIETIES

The American Orchid Society, founded in 1921, is the largest orchid society in the world. It has over 30,000 members worldwide, publishes *Orchids* (previously known as the *American Orchid Society Bulletin*) monthly, and was instrumental in the concept of a World Orchid Conference. The first World Orchid Conference was held in 1954, and assembles every three years in a different city each time. Spectacular displays of orchids are shown, with invited experts presenting papers on orchid-related advances.

The Royal Horticultural Society (then known as the Horticultural Society of London) was founded in 1804 and had important links to Kew Gardens and orchids during this time. Today the RHS has over 200,000 members interested in a wide range of ornamental plants. In 1893, Kew botanist Robert Rolfe established *The Orchid Review*, the oldest publication of its kind.

The *Australian Orchid Review* was established by the Orchid Society of New South Wales in 1936 and is a highly respected and informative periodical. It distributes over 8,000 copies bi-monthly, making it Australia's largest full-color orchid magazine. *Orchids Australia* was established in 1989 and is the official publication of the Australian Orchid Council.

There are orchid societies throughout the world, and many national bodies publish various forms of orchid literature in a range of languages.

Twentieth-century Orchid Enthusiasm

The Great Depression and World War II were the catalysts that crippled the orchid industry in Europe. It was no longer feasible or ethical to heat the vast numbers of glasshouses devoted to orchids, and many superior and distinctive named cultivars of species and historical hybrids were lost forever as the gardeners and enthusiasts were lost to the conflict.

In the decades that followed the two World Wars, there was a resurgence of interest in orchids. Species orchids from around the world especially Mexico, Brazil, Colombia, India, Thailand, and the Philippines were readily available and could be imported at relatively low prices. The development of hybrid orchids of the more horticultural genera such as *Cymbidium*, *Cattleya*, *Paphiopedilum* (then still called *Cypripedium*), *Odontoglossum*, and *Dendrobium* were of more interest to many growers of fine plants. New hybrids quickly replaced older ones that were now horticulturally inferior, and the best of these plants attracted high prices, often the equivalent of hundreds, sometimes thousands, of dollars. It was not until the advent of tissue culture or mericloning, many years later, that these prices began to tumble to more accessible levels.

The first artificial orchid hybrid bloomed in 1856 and was *Calanthe* Veitchii, a combination made at the Veitch nursery between the species *C. vestita* and *C. rosea*. Veitch hybridized orchids across a range of genera and many others followed his lead. Precise records were kept of the various hybrids made, and when they proved successful they were given grex or hybrid names. From 1871, new hybrids were published, along with descriptions, in the *Gardener's Chronicle*. From its inception in 1893, *The Orchid Review* also published new hybrids, a feature it continues today. Frederick Sander compiled a complete listing of up-to-date hybrids and published his first installment of *Sander's List of Orchid Hybrids* in 1906. The Sander family undertook this project until 1961 after which the duties were taken over by the Royal Horticultural Society.

Today, more than 100,000 orchid hybrids have been registered, and their lineages may be traced by the printed volumes of *Sander's List of Orchid Hybrids*, on compact disc, or via the RHS website at www.rhs.org.uk

Slipper Orchids

The 1970s saw the popularity of the Asiatic slipper orchid, *Paphiopedilum*, at an all-time high. The term "slipper orchid" refers to the modified labellum or "pouch" of the flower. Plant collectors searched high and low for rare and unusual orchids from this genus. In 1971, an Indonesian nurseryman Liem Khe Wie had a vivid dream which led him to the elusive "blue" slipper orchid. The realism of his dream was such that he set off with some friends to bring home this mythical plant. His search took him to the thick rainforests of northern Sumatra and the expedition was not without incident, which Khe Wie later documented in the *Orchid Review*. One of the party died after being sucked to death by leeches, and another had to wrestle with a python. The "blue" slipper orchid eluded them and continues to elude discovery, but Khe Wie did find the bright yellow species that was formally described in 1973 as *Paphiopedilum primulinum*.

For slipper orchid enthusiasts, the best was to come. In the late 1970s the superb Chinese trio of the lolly-pink *Paphiopedilum micranthum*, bright yellow *Paphiopedilum armeniacum*, and the green *Paphiopedilum maliopoense* were introduced to the West. They created a sensation when first exhibited and have been used to create a new breed of attractive slipper orchid hybrids.

In 1981, another slipper orchid stole the horticultural headlines, a bright red slipper orchid, later named *Phragmipedium besseae*,

was found in Peru and Ecuador. Also in the 1980s, *Paphiopedilum sanderianum* (the largest flowered of the slipper orchids) was rediscovered in Sarawak, Borneo. Other significant discoveries from that decade include the South American duo of *Epidendrum ilense* and *Pleurothallis viduata*. Both of these were brought into cultivation by Marie Selby Botanical Garden of Sarasota, Florida, in the USA.

of vandaceous orchids and oncidiums primarily for the cut-flower trade, with tens of thousands exported annually.

Major retail orchid nurseries advertise in prominent orchid periodicals. Many have interesting websites, showcasing photographs of their plants, as well as online catalogs. Most carry a wide range of orchids and supplies, while others will specialize in specific genera.

Orchid Nurseries

Commercial orchid nurseries around the developed world supply the majority of flowering plants for local and sometimes international markets. The nurseries supply the demand for flowering pot plants and serve the hobbyist market. In parts of Europe, North America, South Africa, and Australia, large numbers of popular and proven hybrid orchids are mass-produced, with various types flowering throughout the year. There are also hybrids that have been selected because their peak blooming period coincides with major retail high points such as Mother's Day or Christmas—the times when many plants are purchased for gifts. Numerous nurseries in Southeast Asian countries such as Singapore, Thailand, and the Philippines grow large crops

THE GEOGRAPHY OF ORCHIDS

RIGHT *Rocky outcrops provide the ideal conditions for* Dockrillia striolata, *allowing the plant unimpeded drainage, plentiful fresh air, and little competition from other plants.*

Orchids are found almost everywhere in the world, with the exception of the world's deserts, the North and South Poles, and areas of permanent ice and snow. There are certain patterns that orchids follow to adapt to their latitude and prevailing climatic conditions. Variations in rainfall and temperature, especially during the wet and dry seasons, have a great effect on the growth habits of orchids.

Epiphytic Orchids

The highest concentrations of epiphytic orchids occur in the tropics near the Equator, in countries with signficant mountain ranges. Here the highest orchid diversity can be found at mid-altitude, in particular in the northern countries of South America, such as Colombia and Ecuador, and in New Guinea and Indonesia. In these regions, there is little annual variation in length of daylight hours on which the plants depend to photosynthesize. Further from the Equator, there are fewer epiphytic species and this prevalence diminishes yet further in latitudes beyond the Tropics of Capricorn and Cancer.

BELOW *Flowers of the orchid* Cattleya skinneri *on a tree. This is an epiphytic orchid, taking to the treetops for extra light. It is the national flower of Costa Rica.*

Many people imagine steamy rainforests are the ideal home for tree-dwelling orchids. While it is true that a high percentage of orchids grow in tropical conditions, you will also find orchids in other types of forests and woodlands. Trees with rough bark that do not periodically shed or exude tannins and sap generally make good hosts for tree-dwelling orchids. Some, such as a number of *Cymbidium* species, will grow in the rotting heartwood of dead or damaged mature trees.

Over 80 percent of epiphytic orchids grow in the tropics, although this doesn't necessarily mean that they grow in steamy tropical conditions. Many orchids grow in cooler mountainous regions, and altitude therefore plays an important part in their life cycle. Understanding the natural environment of an orchid aides successful cultivation. Epiphytic orchids often grow on trees and branches in rainforests or on twigs overhanging rivers and creeks. Rock outcrops and cliff faces in or near rainforests also provide ideal conditions for orchids. Here the plants receive unimpeded drainage, plentiful fresh air, and rarely suffer from competition from other plants.

Generally, tropical lowland orchid species have a fairly wide distribution. *Bulbophyllum longiflorum* is a typical example, being found from southern Africa, across Southeast Asia, to New Guinea, northeastern Australia, and the Pacific Islands. A high proportion of orchid species that are found in the forests on or near the peaks of high mountains are endemic to that specific area and are found nowhere else. On major peaks such as Mount Kinabalu in Sabah, Borneo, there are literally hundreds of orchids unique to this area. There is a high degree of endemism in the highlands of New Guinea, where there is an explosion of colorful *Dendrobium* and *Bulbophyllum* species, and along the mountain chain of the Andes in South America, home to genera such as *Dracula*, *Epidendrum*, *Lepanthes*, *Lycaste*, *Masdevallia*, *Maxillaria*, and *Pleurothallis*.

Some of the most important orchids in horticulture have their origins in the East. Popular genera such as *Cymbidium*, *Dendrobium*, *Paphiopedilum*, *Phalaenopsis,* and *Vanda* have their centers of distribution in Southeast Asia. The classic cut flower, the *Cattleya* and its relatives, such as *Brassavola*, *Laelia,* and *Sophronitis,* have Brazil in South America as their stronghold. *Brassia*, *Odontoglossum,* and *Oncidium* also have South American origins. Hawaii is referred to as the "Orchid Island" yet is home to only three native terrestrial orchid species.

It is amazing to see the effects of co-evolution taking place half the world away, where genetically unrelated genera have parallel characteristics of a quite separate genus. There are many *Bulbophyllum* species from New Guinea and Indonesia that have individual flowers that are an almost exact match to some of the *Pleurothallis* and *Masdevallia* species from South America. Likewise, the similarity in the blooms of slipper orchids from the genera *Cypripedium*, *Paphiopedilum,* and *Phragmipedium* is remarkable. Here we have orchids that are related, but have evolved in different climates and geographic regions, with completely different growth habits, yet have blooms that are strikingly similar.

Terrestrial Orchids

While a number of deciduous terrestrial orchids occur in the tropics, the majority make their home in temperate climates. In the Northern Hemisphere, the highest concentrations of terrestrial orchids are found from the latitudes of Tropic of Cancer to just within the Arctic Circle, where seven species are found. In the Southern Hemisphere, the numbers are greatest from the latitudes of the Tropic of Capricorn south down to Macquarie Island, where the helmet orchid *Corybas dienemus* grows in

ABOVE Dendrobium parishii *is a deciduous Southeast Asian species that retains its leaves for less than a year. Its growth cycle is dependent on the monsoonal climate it grows in. The fragrant blooms, smelling like raspberries, are produced in small sprays along the naked pseudobulb.*

RIGHT Thelymitra
ixioides *is one of
Australia's famous "Blue
Sun Orchids."
Unfortunately such
spectacular deciduous
terrestrials rarely thrive
in cultivation and tend
to fade away after a
couple of seasons.*

ABOVE
Paphiopedilum
Honey *is a primary
hybrid slipper orchid.
The "slipper" is actually
the labellum, and plays
an important part in the
pollination process.*

subantarctic conditions, some 900 miles (1,500 km) southeast of Tasmania.

Terrestrial orchids have growth, blooming, and dormancy phases that ensure their survival and reproduction in climates that can be harsh for part of the year. In the Northern Hemisphere, their growth cycle is active in late spring and summer, and they become dormant in the fall and winter when the tubers retreat underground to protect themselves from the cold.

The lady's slipper orchid, *Cypripedium*, is a terrestrial orchid. The genus occurs in North America, China, Japan, and parts of Europe including the United Kingdom. Other European examples of terrestrial orchids include the impressive *Dactylorhiza*, *Orchis*, and *Ophrys*. Despite the vast numbers of orchids that are cultivated in North America and throughout Europe, very few are indigenous terrestrial species because they can be difficult to maintain in cultivation over successive seasons without optimum conditions. Native orchids are protected and may be collected only under license. Almost all orchids in commercial cultivation have their natural origins in Southeast Asia and South America.

In the Southern Hemisphere, terrestrial orchids grow and bloom in the cooler and wetter winters, before becoming dormant at the onset of dry and hot summers. In South Africa, this is the case in the genus *Bonetea* and some species of *Disa*.

In Australia, there are a number of spectacular examples of terrestrial orchids. Unfortunately, many are difficult to cultivate because of a complex relationship between the orchid and a specific mycorrhizal fungus that assists the plant in its growth. However, there are a number that are amenable to cultivation, including the greenhoods, *Pterostylis,* and the helmet orchids, *Corybas.* There are also a number of terrestrial species from alpine regions that have a similar life cycle to their relatives in the Northern Hemisphere because they both experience cold winters. Then there are the two unusual species of Australian orchid, from the genus *Rhizanthella,* that spend their lives underground in total darkness.

Terrestrial orchids also grow in the tropics, and these are generally evergreen types that don't retreat underground. Many of these are shade-loving species, with broad leaves and roots that roam around a layer of thick and nutrient-rich leaf litter. Of course, there are exceptions to this rule, with some plants growing in swampy conditions in full sun. The genus *Sobralia* from South America is such an exception.

LEFT *Close-up of a flower of the fly orchid* (Ophrys insectifera). *The flower has evolved to mimic a female flying insect and attract the male to land and, hopefully pollinate, the flower. The orchids* (Orchidaceae) *are one of the most diverse families of flowering plants.*

CONSERVATION OF ORCHIDS

Orchids are threatened in the wild by two main factors—habitat destruction and overexploitation. However, these factors do not affect all orchids equally.

Habitat Destruction

Many orchids hold a precarious existence, with the majority only occurring in geographically restricted areas. This aspect of their biology is their downfall. When the forests are cleared the orchids become extinct. An example of this is *Epidendrum ilense* from Ecuador. Soon after the species was discovered, the forest was cleared and it is now extinct in the wild. Habitat destruction can come in many forms from clearance of forest for agriculture, mining, logging, or urban expansion to the insidious invasion of non-native species that out-compete the local orchid. It can also be on widely different scales, from the felling of a single tree containing hundreds of epiphytes, or from chemical contamination of a local orchid population, to the clearance of huge tracts of forest for timber. Unfortunately habitat destruction is at its greatest in the tropics where the diversity of orchid populations is at its highest.

Habitat destruction does not discriminate between a flamboyant *Cattleya* or a tiny *Pleurothallis*. It is indiscriminate, and because of this, habitat conservation is the single most important aspect of orchid preservation.

Tropical orchids do not generally die of old age, they are often as long-lived as the substrate they grow on, and therefore it is only when this is destroyed that the orchid dies. This may allow some orchids to survive habitat destruction until a time when the forest can regenerate.

It is not the highly showy orchids that are threatened with extinction, as most of these are already entrenched in cultivation. Rather it is the many miniature species, with little horticultural merit, such as *Pleurothallis* and the related *Stelis* from South America that are under threat. In reality, only a small percentage of the world's orchid flora is in cultivation in specialist nurseries, botanical institutions, and private collections.

Orchids form a part of a very delicate and complex ecosystem that can easily become unbalanced. Most orchids have evolved to attract a specific pollinator. If the pollinator disappears the orchid may die out over a period of decades (or perhaps earlier).

RIGHT *View of colonists clearing rainforest from along the banks of the river Amazon (upper right) in Ecuador. This systematic clearing of trees and vegetation from the rainforests has raised concern that countless plant and animal species could be made extinct.*

Despite this, new species continue to be discovered, and a number of "lost" species have been relocated. Ironically, as more and more forests are cleared, people have been able to gain access to areas that were previously inaccessible or required many days' hiking over difficult terrain. A number of rare and unusual species of orchids and other ornamental plants are still being found in countries such as Ecuador and Colombia in South America, and Sumatra, Sarawak, and Sulawesi in Southeast Asia, as well as the highlands of New Guinea. Yet, one wonders how many species have become extinct before they have ever been recorded? It has been estimated that a plant species is lost everyday—obviously, a large percentage of these would be orchids.

While most epiphytic orchids are amenable to cultivation, saprophytic orchids and some terrestrial species are almost impossible to grow using traditional methods, and relocation of plants is rarely successful. Their only chance for survival is preservation of their habitat, hopefully under national park protection.

LEFT AND BELOW
Close-ups of three different species of Pleurothallis *from rainforest in the montane regions of northwestern Ecuador. Ecuador has more than 2,400 species of orchid, and would rival New Guinea in having more species per unit land area than any other country. These botanical orchids are greatly at risk when forests are cleared, as the more "horticulturally attractive" species are often salvaged as a priority, leaving the smaller-flowered orchids to rot on the ground.*

Orchid Collecting

Overcollection of orchids from the wild generally only affects a small number of horticulturally important genera, such as *Paphiopedilum* and *Phalaenopsis.* Orchid populations are often small, therefore collecting can have a serious effect on the survival of the species and in certain cases has led to the extinction of the species in the wild.

Recently a number of exciting new species of *Paphiopedilum* have been discovered in Vietnam. One in particular, *P. vietnamense,* caused a sensation. Large numbers of this species came onto the market illegally, leading to their extinction in the wild less than five years after being discovered. However, it is not just the new rarities that are under pressure. Species that are relatively common in cultivation are also under threat. One case is *Phalaenopsis violacea.* A nursery stripped whole populations of this species from the wild to try to find an unusual white-flowered form.

When they flowered in the nursery, the white-flowered individuals were selected and the remainder discarded.

Community attitude has certainly changed over the past few decades. Over a century ago, countless thousands of orchids were stripped from the forests to satisfy the greed of many of the Victorian orchidists of the day. This action didn't cause any alarm as there was always "plenty more where they came from." As recently as the 1970s there were still nurseries advertising in orchid periodicals that they could supply orchid species in "lots of up to 10,000." In the same decade, an American journal featured the rediscovery of the rare mustard yellow *Paphiopedilum druryi* from southern India. Yet, in the same issue, an advertisement appeared offering the plants at inflated prices. The advertiser had collected every plant he could find in a tiny habitat that was about the size of a ballpark.

All orchids have been placed on Appendix II of CITES (Convention in Trade on Endangered Species of Fauna and

FAR LEFT
Phalaenopsis Candy Twist *'Mandy.'*

LEFT Paphiopedilum druryi *is the rare and rediscovered mustard-yellow flowered slipper orchid from southern India, making it the most remote species in the genus.*

ABOVE *This is a group of nursery-raised plants of the Vietnamese slipper orchid* Paphiopedilum delenatii. *It is vital that rare and threatened species be made available to reputable orchid nurseries, so that the plants can be mass produced and subsequently made available to the orchid-growing public. This ensures an easier plant to grow, at a much-reduced cost, without putting further pressure on wild populations.*

Flora), with species such as *Paphiopedilum* on Appendix I. This international body restricts the trade between member countries of endangered species. Under CITES legislation, the trade in "Appendix I" plants, such as *Paphiopedilum,* was banned. No "wild" plants were to be collected and subsequently exported from the native rainforests. Strict documentation, from both the importing and exporting countries, has to be in place before plants can be transported between countries. Failure to comply can lead to total shipments being confiscated.

The slipper orchids will probably never become extinct because they are entrenched in cultivation in orchid houses throughout the world, from botanical gardens, to nurserymen, to backyard hobbyists and home gardeners. In many ways, they have become highly successful. The well-documented example of *Paphiopedilum delenatii* is such an orchid. Only two or three plants of this delightful pale pink-flowered

Vietnamese species entered a French nurseryman's collection in the 1920s. They were pollinated when in bloom and the seed subsequently sown, with increasing numbers of young seedlings being produced year after year. This went on for decades, and the species has since become entrenched in cultivation around the world. Admittedly, there was little variation between these plants as there was minimal genetic diversity. This was one of the great achievements and success stories for orchid conservationists, until fresh populations were rediscovered in the early 1990s and thousands of plants were ripped out of the forests to such an extent that it is now thought to be extinct in the wild. However, it does illustrate what can be done if the plants are put into the hands of competent nurseries.

The stunning fire engine red *Phragmipedium besseae* was discovered in 1981, and it immediately shot to the top of the "want list." Initially wild-collected plants fetched several hundred U.S. dollars each, whereas nursery-raised plants, of selected higher quality than the original random wild plants, now sell for a fraction of this amount. It is again thanks to professional nurseries, such as the Orchid Zone in California, USA, that vast numbers of rare species are being reproduced. There are now many more plants of *Phragmipedium besseae* around the world than existed in the wild before 1981. Even so, this does not help the species in the wild, since it is now very rare in Peru and Ecuador.

Botanical gardens also have an important role to play. They ensure that rarities are propagated and made available to the wider orchid community. Without them some novelty orchids, such as *Epidendrum ilense* and *Pleurothallis viduata*, may have become extinct. They were originally discovered in Ecuador, South America, on fallen timber that was about to be burned. But unfortunately, since then, they have never been relocated in the wild. All such plants in cultivation, which now number in the hundreds or possibly thousands, have been derived from only one plant of each species.

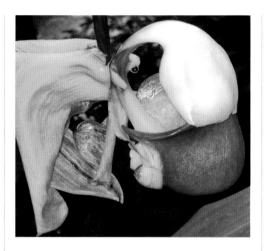

Clearly growers will always want new species as they are discovered, as well as the rarities, and why not? However, this should not be to the detriment of species in the wild. Systems need to be put in place so that orchids can be rapidly propagated, which would require the building of large-capacity greenhouses in the underdeveloped countries where orchids are often found.

The species at real risk are the countless miniature orchids, which were often used as packing for more valuable orchids. These have little commercial value and are only of interest to botanists and species enthusiasts.

SO WHAT CAN YOU DO TO PLAY A PART IN ORCHID CONSERVATION?

- Support nurseries that propagate orchid species from seed. Their stock will not suffer the same "transplant shock" that wild plants endure and should be free of pests and diseases.

- Never buy wild-collected plants.

- Encourage your local orchid society or plant club to use nursery-raised orchid species' seedlings as growing competition plants, instead of hybrid orchids.

- If you have native orchids growing in your local area, help ensure that the habitat is protected. Support can generally be provided by local, state, or national orchid societies as well as dedicated conservation and wildlife organizations.

- Protect information about the location of rare orchids in print or to groups of people. You may unknowingly be adding to the demise of a species.

- Attempt to pollinate rare orchids in your collection. Your local orchid nursery would arrange for the resulting seed capsules to be professionally flasked.

- Grow a number of "botanical" species, such as *Bulbophyllum, Dendrochilum, Pleurothallis,* and *Stelis.* They don't take up much room and their future in the wild is uncertain.

EXHIBITING AND JUDGING ORCHIDS

FAR RIGHT
Phalaenopsis *Brother
Pico Sweetheart.*

RIGHT Cymbidium
Pearl Dawson 'Royale.'

Orchid shows and conferences are held annually in many countries throughout the world. As you experience continued success in growing orchids, you may follow a natural progression to exhibit them at orchid meetings and shows, where they are assessed by qualified orchid judges. This provides another dimension to the enjoyment of orchid cultivation, and motivates growers to improve their skills.

The orchids are generally exhibited in specific classes applicable to a particular genus or family. Classes for popular types of orchids such as cattleyas, cymbidiums, dendrobiums, and paphiopedilums are further divided into categories with emphasis on flower color. First, second, and often third prizes are awarded in each class, taking into account the overall quality of the flowers, their shape and color, as well as presentation.

Orchids of superior quality and/or culture are recognized by major national and regional orchid bodies throughout the world. Panels of accredited judges evaluate the submitted plant and award points (out of

100), in line with recognized judging standards, which assess the flowers' shape, color, size, floriferousness, substance and texture, and presentation. Quality awards tend to increase the commercial (and sometimes financial) value of a plant, as it shows that these are proven species or hybrids with superior blooms and are generally vigorous growing orchids. Only a very small percentage (less than half of one percent) of orchids raised from seed are considered worthy of award consideration.

When selecting orchids from a nursery, catalog, or on the Internet, any awards given to the plants on offer are often highlighted. So if you have a particular interest in *Cattleya* orchids, and you see that one on offer has been awarded, you can expect it to be an above-average selection. However, the year of the award is rarely given due to the fact that awards for orchids were first implemented by the Royal Horticultural Society in London in the late 1800s. So an orchid hybrid awarded in 2000 would in most cases be far superior to one awarded in 1965.

The FCC is the highest quality award and is rarely given. Some judging centers only award a handful over a decade, while larger bodies, such as the American Orchid Society, can award on average one every month or two. Next in descending importance is an AM and HCC. Superior culture and flowering, often with a specimen plant, may be granted an ACC. The AD is used to recognize desirable characteristics such as unusual or intense colors, and there have been instances where perfume has also been recognized. This has been seen with some *Cymbidium* hybrids as well as angraecoid orchids. The AQ is another prestigious award. It is given to a hybrid that displays consistent high quality. Often 12 plants need to be assessed by the judges, but in some systems, only six plants need be presented. The CBM and CBR are similar awards, often granted to orchids that are seldom seen, with desirable or unusual traits that lend them to cultivation.

Divisions or vegetative pieces of awarded orchids are often expensive and highly sought after by enthusiasts. Many of these orchids can be mass-produced by using tissue culture techniques known in the orchid trade as mericloning. The prices then reflect the supply/demand ratio, with the smaller plants a fraction of the cost of the mature plant. Many nurseries sell mericlones of most of the popular genera, with the slipper orchids (*Paphiopedilum* and

Phragmipedium) and *Odontoglossum* being obvious exceptions, as these have proved very difficult to faithfully replicate in numbers in the laboratory.

Nurserymen generally have mericloned the latest and very best hybrid orchid introductions—both in terms of individual blooms and plant vigor. Many of these are also trialed in a range of temperature zones and locations to ensure their worthiness in cultivation. So if you are buying an awarded orchid for the home, you will almost certainly be pleased with your purchase, especially when you first bloom your special plant.

THE NAMES OF AWARDING SOCIETIES

ANOS	Australasian Native Orchid Society
AOC	Australian Orchid Council
AOS	American Orchid Society
CSA	Cymbidium Society of America
DOG	German Orchid Society
JOS	Japan Orchid Society
NSW	Orchid Society of New South Wales
OCNZ	Orchid Council of New Zealand
OCSA	Orchid Club of South Australia
OSCOV	Orchid Societies Council of Victoria
OSNT	Orchid Society of Northern Territory
OSWA	Orchid Society of Western Australia
QOS	Queensland Orchid Society
RHS	Royal Horticultural Society (U.K.)
TASM	Tasmanian Orchid Society
VOC	Victorian Orchid Club

THE MAJOR AWARDS

FCC	First Class Certificate
AM	Award of Merit
HCC	Highly Commended Certificate
ACC	Award of Cultural Commendation
AD	Award of Distinction
AQ	Award of Quality
CBM	Certificate of Botanical Merit
CBR	Certificate of Botanical Recognition

UNDERSTANDING AWARD ABBREVIATIONS

At the international World Orchid Conference (WOC) that is held every three years, Gold, Silver, and Bronze Medals are awarded to the most exceptional prize winning plants that are on display—including cut flowers that are sent from other countries. These are designated by the abbreviations GM, SM, and BM, followed by the specific World Orchid Conference where the award was granted.

For example: GM/16WOC   BM/17WOC

Awarded orchids will have a series of letters after their names, indicating both the award achieved, plus the designated (and internationally recognized) awarding body. These terms are abbreviated.

When written, a slash mark should separate the award from the awarding society, with the award appearing first;

For example: FCC/NSW   AD/VOC   AM/AOS   HCC/RHS

In the event of two awards from one society, or two or more societies granting the same award, it is recommended they be linked with a hyphen. The major award or major society appearing first;

For example: AM-AD/NSW   FCC/AOC-VOC

Whenever an award is published, it should be accompanied by the year in which the award was granted.

For example:
Coelogyne Jannine Banks 'Snow White' HCC/AOC-NSW 1994.

Part Two

CULTIVATION & CARE

There is nothing quite like the thrill of an orchid plant that you have purchased or have received as a gift from a friend. Orchids brighten up the home when in bloom and give your living quarters an exotic ambiance. However the real challenge arises after the orchid has finished blooming, especially if you wish the plant to thrive and provide more flowers in the future. Orchids are easy to grow, and it is surprising how orchid plants can take a certain amount of neglect or less than ideal conditions and yet still flourish. New hybrids raised for pot plants, such as *Phalaenopsis*, are mass-produced to satisfy the growing demand for these flowers in the home. Nurserymen have propagated the most vigorous, colorful, and rewarding varieties for the home gardener and budding orchid enthusiast. With such a variety of orchids available, there are plants suited to window ledges, balconies, greenhouses, and to gardens in frost-free climates.

CARING FOR ORCHIDS INDOORS

Orchids thrive in areas of high humidity and bright light, and while these conditions can sometimes be difficult to achieve in the home, it is possible in areas such as window ledges, bright, warm rooms, and conservatories.

Light and Watering

Select a room that receives light for most of the day. Most orchids prefer bright, indirect lighting, and this should be taken into account when positioning plants in the home. While orchids are unhappy in direct sunlight they do require at least certain light levels, equivalent to about eight hours per day. Avoid placing the plant directly against the window glass as the refraction may burn the plant. Home lighting and house lamps are not appropriate substitutes for daylight, however specialized grow lamps or grow tubes as used in hydroponics or aquariums, do perform the function of sunlight. They do not emit heat so there is not the risk of burning. This form of lighting works best when suspended about 20 inches (50 cm) above the plants.

Pick a spot about 3 feet (90 cm) from the window and choose a sturdy table to support your plants. Sit the pot on a large saucer of pebbles, which will hold just under 1 inch (2.5 cm) of water. This is to help create a little humidity around the plant, however, do not sit the pot in the water, as this will rot its roots.

Once every two weeks, give the plant a thorough watering and wash any dust off the leaves. Use a hose with a rose nozzle or a watering can, liberally flashing the potting medium with water. This drags fresh air to the root system to further freshen the mix.

FAR RIGHT Mist your plants up to five times a day to keep a high level of humidity around them.

RIGHT Place your plant in a tray of pebbles with just under 1 inch (2.5 cm) water. Raise the orchid above the water or the roots will rot. This keeps a high level of humidity around the plant.

Keep an atomizer to hand, preferably with some dilute foliar fertilizer mixed with water (at about a quarter of the strength recommended on the manufacturer's label for ornamental plants), and mist the plant

every time you walk past it. The more you do this the happier your orchid will be, so five times a day is far more beneficial than once a week. This creates a zone of higher humidity around your plant, providing it with perfect growing conditions.

A maximum/minimum thermometer will also let you know exactly what the temperature variation has been. This is most beneficial as you can quickly see exactly how low or how high the temperatures are. This allows you to get an accurate reading of how hot or cold a particular location is, and if necessary plants may be moved to a more suitable position.

Easy Care Orchids

Phalaenopsis hybrids, or "moth orchids," are among the most majestic flowers on the planet, and they are the best orchids to grow indoors. They are compact growing, will accept a range of lighting conditions, and enjoy a temperature range that is also pleasant for humans! Their flower spikes should only be cut off if they have turned brown and died. As long as this stem is green, there is the potential for more flowers to be produced along dormant eyes of the peduncle—which is the part of the flowering stem between the plant and the first flower.

RIGHT *Paphiopedilum, or slipper orchids, are easy to grow at home. However, unlike Phragmipediums they prefer shadier conditions.*

BELOW *Phalaenopsis plants growing in a greenhouse. These plants are popular with orchid collectors because they are easy to care for.*

The South American *Phragmipedium* slipper orchids also make excellent indoor plants, and they are easy to care for. Phragmipediums prefer higher light than most Paphiopedilums and much more water. The root systems on *Phragmipedium* are generally more extensive and finer than the few very thick roots that occur in *Paphiopedilum*, which in the wild grows in moist conditions.

A number of orchid growers and enthusiasts started experimenting with growing Phragmipediums in the home in the early 1990s. They chose to position them on bright window ledges which did not receive full, direct sunlight, placing them in containers that held about 2 inches (5 cm) of water. They were kept in this position throughout the year. This was against the generally accepted advice that previously advocated a mix with a perfect drainage system that dried out between waterings. Surprisingly, the orchids flourished and bloomed throughout the year.

Paphiopedilum slipper orchids will not tolerate sitting in water, and prefer shadier conditions to phragmipediums. Keep their growing medium just on the damp side and frequently mist the foliage to keep the plant healthy. Paphiopedilums have blooms that can last for long periods, up to three months with some of the hybrid types.

ORCHIDS IN TERRARIUMS

Miniature orchid species can be grown successfully in glass fish tanks—modified into terrariums. Cool lighting tubes should to be connected to a timer to control the amount of light the plants receive. Generally, a "day" period of 14 hours is best employed for most genera.

A layer of pebbles or gravel is placed on the bottom of the tank, to a depth of about 2 inches (5 cm) with a water level kept at about 1 inch (2.5 cm). The potted plants sit on top of the gravel, which allows water levels to be retained in the tank, without the base of the pots sitting in the water. Do not place this enclosure where it will be subject to direct sunlight, as the temperature may rise to unacceptable levels that could put stress on the plants.

Orchids can be mounted on the back and side walls of your growing chamber. You will be surprised how many miniature and small-growing orchids can be grown in a 3 x 1 foot (100 x 30 cm) fish tank.

Use atomizers to water the mounted plants, misting the potted plants at the same time. This is best done daily during the spring and summer, to every three or four days in winter and fall. To give potted plants a proper watering, it's better to take them out of the terrarium so that they can drain properly before they are placed back in the tank. As a guide, these potted orchids should be watered once a week in autumn, once every ten days in winter, and twice a week in spring and summer (when most of these orchids would be in active growth). The plants should retain a high humidity level due to the water at the bottom of the tank.

Some of the recommended orchids for glass tanks include *Aerangis*, smaller-growing *Angraecum*, *Bulbophyllum*, miniature *Dendrobium*, smaller-growing *Maxillaria*, *Masdevallia*, compact *Oncidium*, *Pleurothallis*, *Polystachya*, *Promenaea*, *Restrepia*, *Sarcochilus*, *Sophronitis,* and *Stelis*.

ABOVE *Mist miniature orchids, such as this* Stelis, *daily in the summer months to keep them at a high humidity. Regular misting helps them flourish during the warmer, dryer months.*

LEFT *Close-up of an orchid,* Maxillaria rufescens, *from the forest of northwestern Ecuador. This is just one of the many types of miniature orchid that are recommended for growing in terrariums.*

Orchids in Conservatories

Conservatories, sun lounges, and glassed-in patios and decks can provide conditions similar to that of a glasshouse, and offer an ideal home for many types of orchids, such as cattleyas, cymbidiums, epidendrums, vandaceous orchids, zygopetalums, and many larger growing dendrobiums. A conservatory is also an ideal environment for palms, bromeliads, ferns, and a host of other ornamentals, which are ideal companion plants to orchids. Do not place the orchids in direct sunlight or against the glass during the warmer months when they could scorch, or conversely when they could be chilled in the colder months.

The orchids will be happiest on wide trays with a pebble bed, so that water can be kept in the trays without the pots being submerged. A tray depth of 2 inches (5 cm) would be ideal, with the water level kept to at least 1 inch (2.5 cm).

Regularly mist the plants with a fertilizer/water mix, at a quarter of the rate as recommended by the manufacturer, to keep the humidity levels high. This must be done more frequently during the warmer months when an orchid's growth rate is at its highest. In the winter months its growth slows down, with some species entering a dormant phase, so watering should be kept to a minimum.

Orchids that you may be growing in outside areas or shadehouses can be brought into the home when in bloom to brighten up a room. They can be kept indoors for the life of the blooms, but if you are going away for a few days give the plants a thorough watering before you leave. For longer vacations, arrangements should be made to have your plants either housed elsewhere (if you only have a handful) or arrange for someone to water them in your absence.

ABOVE *Cymbidiums are easy to grow at home and come in a wide range of beautiful colors due to extensive cultivation. They last in bloom for over a month, and the flowers are highly and sweetly fragrant.*

ORCHIDS IN THE GARDEN

ABOVE *A* Telipogon *orchid.*

BELOW Oncidium nubigenum *grows at high elevations in the South American Andes Mountains.*

Orchids can certainly make an impact in an established garden. Only hardy and durable orchids should be selected and there are many types that can be grown on trees and rocks, but only in frost-free areas. The number of species available to grow in your garden increases as you move into warmer climates.

Orchids on Trees

Epiphytic orchids grow well on trees, especially on those with a rough bark texture that doesn't flake or exude resin.

Some of the best garden trees for "orchidscaping" include coral trees (*Erythrina* sp.), frangipani (*Plumeria* sp.), *Jacaranda*, *Liquidambar*, English oak (*Quercus robur*), *Camellia*, *Magnolia*, *Banksia*, *Melaleuca*, *Callistemon*, *Grevillea robusta*, and citrus fruit

trees (*Citrus* sp.). The trunk and main branches are the best places to plant your epiphytic orchids. Larger plants may be attached to the trunks of mature palm trees that have a fibrous texture.

To select a site for the orchid plant, first choose from either the main trunk or a secure branch, and remember that most orchids like to be out of direct summer sunlight. Deciduous trees are ideal, as they let in plenty of quality light in winter and provide shade during the heat of summer.

Tie the orchids on firmly, after removing the plant from the pot and shaking off the mix. Pantyhose are ideal for tying and much better than plastic-coated wire which can cut into branches or orchid roots. Position a pad of *Sphagnum* moss at the roots to provide moisture while the plant is establishing itself. The orchid appreciates regular watering, every two or three days, at least for the first six months. After that, they can rely on rain water. During extended dry periods, a thorough watering with the garden hose should be given to the plants once a week.

Orchids on Rocks

Sedimentary rocks, such as sandstone and conglomerate, and rocks of volcanic origin (basalts and granites) are the best hosts for orchids in a rockery. Large boulders are preferable to a grouping of small rocks. Limestone may also be used, but concrete is unsatisfactory because the lime content is too strong for the plant's roots. Select sites that provide some shade during the full heat of the day. Most orchids suitable for tree culture will also grow well on rocks, as many species can be found growing in the wild as both epiphytes and lithophytes. If slugs and snails are a problem, baits will need to be laid during damp weather; otherwise they will feast on the succulent orchid roots.

Orchids in Borders

A number of terrestrial orchids are suited to border planting, but watch out for pests such as slugs and snails. Hybrid cymbidiums may also be grown on elevated beds of bark and compost with a ring of larger rocks around them to keep the mixture in. Suitable genera for frost-free temperate climates include *Bletilla*, *Calanthe*, some reed-stem *Epidendrum*, *Pleione*, *Sobralia*, and *Thunia*. In warmer climates *Arundina*, *Neobenthamia*, *Phaius*, *Spathoglottis*, and terete-leafed vandas may also be grown.

ABOVE Dendrobium speciosum *subsp.* hillii *grown as a garden plant, attached to a tree in a frost-free climate.*

ORCHIDS IN A SHADEHOUSE

A backyard shadehouse, whether in temperate, subtropical, or tropical climates, can accommodate a range of ornamental plants such as ferns, small palms, bromeliads, hoyas, rhododendrons, clivias, *Nepenthes* pitcher plants, plus a range of other foliage and flowering plants. All these plants are perfect companions to orchids, as they enjoy the same conditions, and many grow alongside orchids in the wild. A shadehouse (or bushhouse) is a well-ventilated structure, which while providing shade also maintains higher humidity than outside. In summer it will be a few degrees cooler than the outside temperature, while in winter it provides protection from mild frosts.

The best place to locate a shadehouse is on a site that receives maximum winter sun. It is a lot easier to apply shade than to increase light. Always make the house larger than you plan, as you will be surprised how quickly you fill it. Most shadehouses are built of water pipe and are connected by

metal clips designed for this type of construction. Treated timbers can also be used—often it is a question of esthetics. Plan to have a high roof. This allows for a greater volume of circulating air and offers more hanging options for plants as you create different levels within the shadehouse.

There are various types of shadecloth available, but the knitted types in dark green are recommended. The grade of shadecloth depends on surrounding conditions, such as neighboring trees or buildings. In a larger shadehouse, you can have two or three different grades of shadecloth (running east to west) and should bench the plants

accordingly. In exposed or very hot situations, you may wish to add another layer of shadecloth during the summer. Generally 70 percent coverage of a shadehouse is recommended for a mixed collection, which provides a cooler, semi-shaded environment.

Cover your benches in weld mesh on which to place your potted plants. Weld mesh does not deteriorate and allows for air circulation around the plants. It can be purchased in sheets and cut with bolt cutters or an angle grinder. Line the cut areas of mesh along the walkway with plastic tubing, to protect your clothing and skin as you work at the bench.

Position the benches slightly lower than "hip height," so you do not need to bend down to attend to your plants. There is also more humidity closer to the floor at this level, and it is therefore often a little cooler in the summer. It also gives more room to hang plants above.

If you intend to grow many mounted plants, you could install an "A frame" (also made out of weld mesh) in the middle of your shadehouse. A few panels on the western and southern walls will give you added space for hanging plants and help reduce the impact of the stronger winds from those directions. A few runs of barbed wire along the top of the house will give you yet more hanging space.

It's better to have an earth floor because this will reduce the humidity in the house and, if the conditions are right, ferns will grow under the bench. Sawdust and wood shavings may also be used in thick layers. Pavers or a generous layer of blue metal is recommended for the walkways to avoid a slippery or potentially muddy surface.

A misting system provides the finishing touch to the shadehouse. While it cannot replace hand-watering your collection, it is effective in maintaining humidity throughout the year and cooling the plants on warm summer evenings. This is especially helpful to enthusiasts growing orchids in countries with hotter climates.

LEFT *A group of modern* Cymbidium *hybrids are easily grown in shadehouses in temperate climates, coming in a wide range of colors. As an added bonus, the long-lasting blooms are also fragrant.*

ORCHIDS IN A GLASSHOUSE

The installation of a glasshouse (greenhouse) will markedly increase the range of orchid genera that can be successfully grown and enjoyed. If you live in an area that experiences a lot of frosts and sub-zero temperatures, you will want to invest in a glasshouse to grow your orchids. Not only will a glasshouse keep your plants protected in winter, but it will be effective in keeping montane orchids cooler in summer, especially if you install an evaporative cooler.

A glasshouse can be built from glass sheeting, fiberglass panels, or sheets of laserlite and may also be lined with clear or bubble plastic to assist insulation. There are many prefabricated glasshouse models available, in a range of styles and sizes. However, most of these will not have a high enough roof. To overcome this drawback

and raise the height, prepare a sturdy brick and concrete base, and bolt the glasshouse supports into the structure. Altenatively, you could excavate and lower the floor of the glasshouse to increase the functional height and volume of air.

Select a bright, sunny aspect if you intend concentrating on lowland tropical orchids, such as dendrobiums, cattleyas, and vandaceous genera. A shadier position would be preferable for masdevallias, paphiopedilums, *Phalaenopsis,* and most montane species. If you are unsure, go for the sunny site, as you can always increase the shading. Try to have the entrance on the southern side—that way you can leave the door open periodically to let in fresh air without the worry of direct sunlight hitting the plants.

While shadecloth may be draped directly over the glasshouse, it is preferable to build or modify a frame around the glasshouse for this purpose. As you construct your frame, leave a gap of 12 inches (30 cm) from the roof, to allow airflow between the shading and the house. Cover this with chicken wire before attaching the shadecloth. This will protect your glasshouse from hailstorms and flying debris. A spare layer of shadecloth is useful in the summer and can be removed once the warmer months are over.

For the interior of your glasshouse, weld mesh benches are the best choice, installed between knee and hip height. Finer wire mesh (such as chicken wire) can be laid on top of this to provide a base to stop smaller plants falling through or tipping over, although seedlings can be grouped in small wire or plastic trays. Mesh frames should be placed and securely fastened, at a slight angle, to accommodate mounted plants. Whereas, earthen floors provide perfect conditions for orchids and ferns. Use blue metal as a base to keep the weeds down.

BELOW *A group of* Miltoniopsis *hybrids, showcasing the range of colors and styles within this group.*

Always hand-water in a glasshouse, using a rose fitting for deep watering or a fine mist spray to dampen mounted plants and their roots, and to wet the leaves of potted plants. This increases the overall humidity. Misting systems are effective in larger glasshouses, as long as they are kept away from the electronics. Many growers and nurseries install under-bench misting systems to maintain or increase humidity and also to reduce the temperature during warmer months without wetting the orchids.

There should be plenty of air movement in your glasshouse, and strategically placed ceiling or oscillating fans will keep your orchids happy. An exhaust fan is useful for extracting hot air during the warmer months. However, the combination of electricity and water can be dangerous so ensure that fittings and switches are installed by a qualified electrician and that they are waterproof.

In order to heat a small glasshouse during the cooler months, a domestic fan heater (with internal thermostat) will suffice for a few winters before burning out. Many nurseries have had success with oil heaters, hot water systems, and professional glasshouse heaters (that blow hot air or use radiant heat). Some are more energy efficient than others. Major suppliers can be found through advertisements in horticultural magazines.

Some tropical orchids can be more difficult subjects to bloom (or even grow) when moved latitudes away from their native home, even when their optimum temperature requirements are provided. This is because we cannot always replicate the lengths of daylight experienced by equatorial plants. Some of the larger-growing lowland vandaceous orchids fall into this category, as do many of the impressive tall-growing *Dendrobium* species. By the time they are receiving sufficient light, and their triggers for growth or flowering begin, the days shorten and often flowering is aborted. They produce their new growths (which may take two years to

mature) in response to 12 hours of sunlight. Plants grown in heated glasshouses in temperate climates are always a few months behind. During winter, when daylight hours are fewer, they just stop growing (which they don't do in the wild), and are more susceptible to rot, leaving you with a weaker plant. Realistically, these plants are best cultivated in the tropics.

The function of a glasshouse is not only to heat plants in colder months, but also to cool them in the hotter months. This can be achieved with the installation of an evaporative cooler. This modifies the atmosphere to make it conducive to the culture of cool climate genera, such as *Odontoglossum, Masdevallia, Dracula* and the colorful New Guinean dendrobiums, that dislike high summer temperatures.

ABOVE Phalaenopsis Fagen's Fireworks, *one of the popular moth orchids.*

TEMPERATURE REQUIREMENTS

When discussing the temperature ranges of orchids, emphasis tends to be placed on their minimum winter requirements with not much said about the summer temperatures. While it is true that there are lowland tropical orchids that will suffer or even die if the temperature drops below a certain point for an extended length of time, there are also montane species that dislike high temperatures during summer. Most of the world's epiphytic orchids grow in mountainous regions near the Equator where the plants experience a narrow corridor of temperature variation. Generally the temperature rarely falls below 50°F (10°C) nor rises above 78°F (26°C), an annual variance of only 28°F (16°C). These are ideal conditions for the species that make their homes in these parts. However, in cultivation, we tend to grow vastly different types of orchids in a handful of microclimates. Luckily, most orchids are adaptable and are able to withstand both cool and warm temperatures.

Very few epiphytic or lithophytic orchids can handle temperatures at or below

THE TEMPERATURE REQUIREMENTS FOR ORCHIDS

COOL GROWING

These plants should be kept cool in summer
Winter: daytime minimum 54°F (12°C)/nighttime minimum 41°F (5°C).
Summer: daytime maximum 50°F (10°C)/nighttime maximum 86°F (30°C).

INTERMEDIATE GROWING

These plants can stand cool temperatures for short periods
Winter: daytime minimum 64°F (18°C)/nighttime minimum 50°F (10°C).
Summer: daytime maximum 50°F (10°C)/nighttime minimum 95°F (35°C).

WARM GROWING

These plants can bear high temperatures provided humidity is high
Winter: daytime minimum.
Summer: daytime maximum 75°F (24°C) with a nighttime minimum of 59°F (15°C), susceptible to temperatures below 50°F (10°C), these plants can bear high temperatures provided humidity is high.

CHOOSE THE ORCHID THAT SUITS THE CONDITIONS OF YOUR HOME

- *Paphiopedilum* and *Phalaenopsis* are perfect for growing in the home. Place in a well-lit spot (but not direct sun) and a minimum temperature of 60°F (16°C) with a rise of 10°F (6°C) in the day. During the summer months keep the temperature below 90°F (32°C).

- *Cattleya, Miltoniopsis,* and *Zygopetalum* will all thrive if given a minimum temperature of 55°F (13°C) with a rise of 10°F (6°C) in the day. Place in a shaded spot. During the summer months keep the temperatures below 85°F (29°C).

- *Odontoglossum, Odontioda,* and *Cymbidium* will be happy in a heated conservatory or glasshouse with a minimum night temperature of 50°F (10°C), with a rise of 10°F (6°C) in the day. During the summer keep the temperature below 80°F (27°C). Place out of direct sun. Place cymbidiums in a shady spot outside during the summer months.

freezing for longer than a few hours. Frost is an enemy of orchids and can kill plants if they have been kept moist. It is important for the plants to have an increase in temperature during the day, ideally in conjunction with clear skies. Water orchids in the morning on sunny days, as you must ensure the plants will dry before sundown. Many healthy plants will endure brisk temperatures (down to 36°F/2°C) for three or four hours in the morning as long as the day temperature gets to around 59°F (15°C). Make sure the plants are dry by evening and keep an eye on the weather maps and forecasts. Clear skies, a full moon, and no wind during winter months are the first indicators of the possibility of frost.

Many deciduous terrestrial orchids from temperate climates have adapted to cold winter temperatures. They grow and flower in the fall and winter and remain dormant underground (as tubers) during the hot and often dry summers.

Many high-altitude or montane species (from 4,921 feet/1,500 m above sea level and higher) never experience high temperatures in the wild. Anything above 86°F (30°C) is uncommon. It is imperative during heat waves to keep humidity high in the orchid growing area, keep the floor damp, and only water your plants once the sun is off them. Adding an extra layer of shadecloth can also help to lower the temperature and prevent scorching.

Most orchids grown in the home will experience temperatures that we as humans find most comfortable—generally from 57°F (14°C) to 86°F (30°C) would be the average range for inside the house. This is also the ideal range for most epiphytic orchids. Heaters and coolers can be used to regulate these temperatures, but the humidity in the home is significantly less than that experienced by orchids in the forests and those in a glasshouse. To compensate for this, place your plants in a suitable position and pay careful attention to their watering requirements. Regular misting of your plants will ensure successful cultivation, especially in the hotter months.

WATERING

Watering is the most fundamental task for gardeners and a minefield for calamity. When dealing with orchids many novices approach it with hesitation. It is imperative that the plant's root system is allowed to drain freely and quickly and that there is constant movement of fresh air. Watering is a science that can only be mastered with practice, as everyone has different plants, conditions, and lifestyles.

Plants in active growth need more water than when they are in a dormant state. Ensure the plants get a "deep" watering, with excess water flowing liberally out of the drainage holes, as opposed to a splash with a watering can or hose. All plants require more moisture in summer than in winter and many orchids require a dry period as part of their annual growth cycle in the cooler months, and this dormancy needs to be respected.

Channel rainwater off the roof of the family home, garage, and any orchid houses with a solid roof, and into a water tank to use for your indoor species. This is particularly important in areas where the quality of the town water supply is questionable. Many local supplies have high concentrations of chlorine, which can be poisonous to sensitive plants, including orchids, and will quickly kill growing *Sphagnum* moss. If practical, store this water for at least 24 hours in an open vessel before using on your orchids. During this time, the chlorine should have dissipated.

Misting systems can also be installed in the orchid house. Basic systems (including plastic tubing, nozzles, and hose attachments) are relatively inexpensive, easily installed, and an excellent inclusion. You can even have its operation computer-controlled or on a timer that snaps onto the tap. Misters are primarily used to increase humidity and cool the temperature around the plants. Regardless of how many nozzles you install, there will always be dry patches. This is due to different-sized plants, as some will have foliage that shields other plants. There is more chance of uniform coverage if there is air circulation. Depending on the area to be covered (and size of the collection), it may be wise to install several runs, with the number of nozzles governed by your water pressure.

Ideally, nothing can compare to hand watering, where you also get the opportunity to inspect your plants and take any action required if you spot a problem. A rose nozzle delivers a gentle shower of water to your plants without blasting them away. There are also extension wands that are ideal for watering hanging pots and baskets, as well as mounted plants that are hung up high in the orchid house. Some hose attachments deliver an ultra fine mist, which is most useful for dampening the foliage and quenching mounted orchids.

In summer when a thunderstorm is on its way, plants will enjoy heavy rain that carries additional nitrogen due to the chemical reaction caused by lightning. However, the downside is the strong winds that often accompany storms. A few days after such a downpour, have a good look at the root systems of your plants. You will find that they have longer green root-tips and the foliage has added luster. You will also be surprised to discover that many of the "one-day wonders" (orchids which have blooms that generally last for less than 24 hours) will initiate inflorescences which should bloom in about nine or ten days' time. This is a

ABOVE *A portable watering can and nozzle such as this is ideal for hand watering and misting mounted and hanging orchids.*

response to a sudden change in atmospheric pressure (as happens during thunderstorms), rather than to a drop in temperature often credited for instigating flowering. Orchids that respond in this manner include some sections of *Dendrobium*, *Diplocaulobium*, some *Eria*, *Flickingeria*, and *Grastidium*. It is not uncommon to have a whole suite of different species in bloom on the same day, or a week or so after a storm.

ABOVE *Hand watering orchids is the best approach, as you can also check for any problems as you water.*

FERTILIZING

There are many brands of fertilizer on the market and the two main choices are organic (natural) and inorganic (chemical). Fertilizer may be applied in dry or liquid form. Organic fertilizers can vary in quality depending on the raw materials and the time of year it is produced. Chemical fertilizers are more consistent as their contents can be measured and replicated exactly. A good option is to alternate between both types of fertilizer.

The primary elements for plant growth are nitrogen (N), phosphorus (P), and potassium (K); these three components are termed NPK. Secondary elements such as calcium, magnesium, and sulfur are also important to plant growth. Other trace elements including boron, manganese, copper, zinc, and iron are required in minute quantities.

Use a high nitrogen (N) based fertilizer from late spring to early fall, when most orchids are in active growth. The nitrogen helps the growth of the plant and gives it a green luster during a period of high temperatures and strong light. For a mixed collection, a suitable fertilizer would have an NPK ratio of 22-8-12 or similar.

From mid-fall to spring, a fertilizer that promotes healthy roots, boosts the quality of the flowers, and overall strengthens the plant should be used. This has a lower nitrogen content, as most genera have slowed their growth rate considerably and are now concentrating on flowering. A suitable fertilizer would have a higher potassium (K) component and an NPK ratio of 12-12-20 or similar. There are many variations available, and it is imperative that the manufacturers' instructions are adhered to for application. Higher-than-recommended concentrations of fertilizer will not make the plants grow faster, and you will run the risk of burning the roots and the foliage. Many growers feed their plants less than the manufacturers' recommended rate, but apply it more frequently. There is an old saying among growers of cymbidiums— "weekly but weakly."

Every few weeks, flush the pots out with lots of pure water to remove any excess salts, then repeat this an hour later, to wash out any remaining dissolved salts.

For a small collection, a watering can with a rose nozzle is perfect for fertilizing your plants. This way you also know exactly how much food you are giving your plants. Make sure the ingredients are fully dissolved before applying—initially adding a dash of hot water will accelerate the process. Many garden centers now sell plant feeders (with a screw-on jar to hold the fertilizer), complete with rose nozzle, which snaps onto the end of the hose. Water mixes with the contents and dispenses the fertilizer for about 15 minutes—very handy if you are fertilizing a small section of your collection.

For a larger collection, a fertilizer proportioner can be attached to the hose at the faucet. As the water comes

ABOVE *Some orchid nurseries create their own fertilizer. McBean's Orchid Nursery in England produces and sells its own brand of fertilizer.*

RIGHT *Watering cans with a rose nozzle are ideal for watering and fertilizing orchids.*

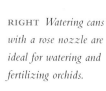

from the faucet, it siphons fertilizer from the pre-made concentrated mix in the proportioner.

Because orchids don't grow as fast as annuals and most foliage plants, the fertilizer rate may be reduced to half that recommended by the manufacturer. It is best to sway on the side of too little fertilizer than too much. However, some vigorous orchids can be safely fertilized at full strength during their active growing period.

These "heavy feeders" include cymbidiums and dendrobiums. Manure pellets and slow-release inorganic fertilizers (with the chemicals inside tiny balls) can also be applied during the growing season. These release their nutrients over a few months. Organic types can be applied to the surface of the mix, while it is best to slightly cover the tiny beads of the inorganics, as they have a tendency to deteriorate quickly when exposed to sunlight.

BELOW *Cymbidiums are "heavy feeders" and can be fertilized at full strength during their active growing period.*

GROWING ORCHIDS IN POTS

Orchids are grown in pots for convenience and practicality. They accommodate the plants' root systems while retaining moisture, and are also relatively inexpensive, as well as being easy to transport and display. Many are also reusable, as long as they are cleaned in a mild bleach solution before use.

With the wide range of pots available, it's important that you select sturdy pots with generous drainage holes. Today, plastic pots are most frequently used, and they are available in a variety of sizes, styles, colors, and depths.

Try to house plants in the same pot size, especially if they are together on a bench. It looks tidier, and the pots should dry out at the same time so they can safely be watered together.

Seedling orchids have the same cultural requirements as adults of the same genus. The only difference is that seedlings have a preference for shadier conditions until they reach a mature size. Seedlings also enjoy being repotted more frequently than mature plants, and usually need to be repotted every 12 months into fresh potting medium.

Remove weeds from the pots and the floor of your orchid houses. If these are left to seed, they will spread. Pull them out by hand using a pair of tweezers for stubborn weeds with taproots. Weeds under the bench may be carefully sprayed, in still conditions, with an herbicide. Beware of weeds in hanging baskets, as these can disperse their seeds quite a distance from above. If you are diligent, it is possible to eliminate weeds.

TERRACOTTA POTS

Before the introduction of plastic pots, traditional terracotta pots were the nursery standard for decades. They were deep pots that required "crocking" (placing broken pieces of terracotta up to a third of the height of the pot to assist drainage). They are expensive, heavy, and invariably have poor drainage holes. However, these can be enlarged with a few gentle blows of a hammer at the edge of the hole. Another disadvantage is that orchids with thick roots (such as cattleyas and vandaceous orchids) cling tightly to the inside and outside of the pot, and the roots can be damaged when removed. Dry out the plant and its potting medium over a few days, so that the roots and mix slightly contract. This will make the job of removing the plant much easier, minimizing damage to the root system.

Despite this, there are many orchids that enjoy life in terracotta pots. Some of the squat designs, coupled with round drainage holes on the sides of the pot, have proved popular with medium-sized monopodial orchids, such as the rock-growing *Laelia* species and dendrobiums. The roots will run over the pot's surface and through the drainage holes. These orchids are happy to spend their lives undisturbed, simply clambering over the container. This is fine, until the mix deteriorates and needs to be replaced. It must also be noted that orchids in terracotta pots will dry out much faster than their counterparts in plastic containers.

There are two ways to deal with a deteriorated mix. The first option is to hold the pot and tip the plant upside down, using your fingers to dislodge any stray compost. The second involves using a jet of water to wash away the old material, but not too strong as to dislodge or damage the roots.

New potting medium (generally bark) is placed into the cavity that has been left. This is best done while the plant is in active growth. You will find orchids treated this way will respond with renewed vigor.

STANDARD PLASTIC POTS

There are many orchids (terrestrial or semi-terrestrial) with an extensive or deep root system that prefer standard-sized pots. The large-flowered orchids or cymbidiums, plus many of the "intermediate" types certainly prefer the deeper pots. However, most growers and nurseries use the squat style pots for "miniature" cymbidiums and for some of the less vigorous "intermediates." There are other types of orchids that favor the deeper pots, including *Phaius*, *Sobralia*, and some of the very tall growing dendrobiums (such as *Dendrobium. fimbriatum*, *D. moschatum*, and *D. pulchellum*). Add a handful of large pebbles to the bottom of the pot of tall growing plants to boost its weight and stability.

SQUAT PLASTIC POTS

These are arguably the most popular pots used for the cultivation of most orchids. Generally they are about two-thirds the height of standard pots and their diameter exceeds their depth. The advent of squat pots has made redundant the old practice of

BELOW *Although terracotta pots are esthetically pleasing, the standard and squat plastic pots provide better drainage.*

"crocking" pots. Most epiphytic and lithophytic orchids run their roots along tree branches and rock surfaces in the wild, yet when confined to pots, the initial roots often descend at a 45° angle. These roots eventually hit the sides and are forced to spiral deeper into the pot. Some even manage to sprout through the drainage holes. Most of the active root growth will be confined to the top 4 inches (10 cm) of the potting medium. When repotting many cattleyas and dendrobiums, you will notice that the roots have spiraled many times and have become quite long, but there won't be much active root growth in the center of the pot. This is quite normal and is a pattern mirrored by many orchid genera.

BELOW Orchids such as odontoglossums and phalaenopsis thrive in plastic pots, which give the roots room to grow. They also allow ample drainage.

SAUCERS

Terracotta saucers are very popular for creeping miniature orchids, vigorous bulbophyllums, some *Pterostylis*, and are ideal for the culture of *Pleione* species and its hybrids. These are orchids with a relatively shallow root system, which spreads just under the surface of the potting medium. There are also manufacturers who make plastic saucers, but these have few (if any) drainage holes. However these can easily be added using a soldering iron.

HANGERS

Orchids in pots are often better displayed (and often grow with improved vigor) when suspended. In this position, the plants

receive more light and air circulation than plants on a bench. It should also be noted that the humidity is slightly lower. The plants can be hung on runs of barbed wire. Fishing swivels (installed between the hanger and another small wire hook) can also be used for specimen plants that are growing in many directions, which allow the plant to rotate when watering.

The most readily available hangers are the "clip-on" three-pronged plastic hangers, with hooks that clip onto the rim of the pot. Insist on black, as colored hangers quickly deteriorate in sunlight and become brittle and break within a year. They are suitable for plastic only and are useful for pot sizes from 5 to 8 inches (12.5 cm to 20 cm). Only sturdy wire hangers should be used for larger pots, preferably with four prongs.

Long hooks are made in a range of sizes from strong wire. The loop fits under the rim of the pot, with a long straight piece 12 to 20 inches (30 to 50 cm) long above the pot level, ending in a hook. Both plastic and terracotta pots are suitable for these hangers. If your growing area has a high enough roof, they are sturdy enough to have other plants "hooked" underneath. If in doubt about what size to get, choose the larger diameter—you can always place an empty pot in the loop and prop the smaller pot with bark, pebbles, or moss. Obviously, it is best to try to obtain a range of sizes, as you will find them very handy. Plus, unlike plastic hooks, the stainless steel won't deteriorate.

Potted plants can also be hung on "A-frames" using customized wire hangers in a range of sizes. These consist of a loop of strong wire that fits snugly under the rim of the pot. Two metal hooks attach this hook to the vertical wire mesh. This works best for smaller pots, from tubes 2 inches (5 cm) up to 5 inches (12.5 cm). Again, both plastic and terracotta pots are suitable for these hangers.

GROWING ORCHIDS IN BASKETS

ABOVE *Stanhopeas are obvious candidates for basket culture, this epiphytic species is one of the forms of* Stanhopea oculata.

There is no doubt that orchids grown in baskets enhance an orchid collection. The most common types of container to use are square timber-slatted baskets, often made of teak, cedar, or other untreated hardwood, and wire baskets. Some orchids need to be grown in baskets so their blooms can be displayed to full potential. Stanhopeas are an obvious example, with their stiff, descending flower spikes. It is desirable to select plants that can be left undisturbed in their baskets for many years

Species with long arching or pendulous inflorescences, such as *Coelogyne*, *Coryanthes*, *Cuitlauzina*, some *Cymbidium* species and hybrids, and *Gongora* are best grown and displayed in either wooden or wire baskets.

Orchids with a pendant growth habit are more frequently grown on slabs but if the conditions are too dry, they can be grown in baskets, where there is more moisture available to the root system. Many *Dockrillia* species and hybrids, as well as the pendulous dendrobiums, are good candidates for small baskets.

Timber baskets are exclusively used for supporting vandas and related monopodial genera with thick roots, often without bark or other material being used. In the tropics, the seedlings are planted on the bottom of the basket. Initially, the roots ramble and attach themselves to the timber, and then as they become older the roots elongate and hang vertically below the basket. Plants grown this way require little maintenance and can be grown undisturbed for many years.

Stanhopeas are superb candidates for hanging baskets, with their stiff, descending flower spikes. They punch their flower "spears" down through the growing medium hoping to emerge into fresh air, and then they burst into bloom. If the spike hits the bottom of a plastic pot or a wooden slat, it will just rot away. Plant your *Stanhopea* in a wire basket, inserting a thin lining of paperbark (*Melaleuca* sp.) or teased coconut fiber to hold your potting medium. Do not use coconut liners, as the liners are too dense for the *Stanhopea* spikes to penetrate.

Orchids in Baskets

1 *Once your orchid has grown large enough to be placed in a hanging basket (like this* Coelogyne cristata *above), let the potting medium dry out so that the plant can be easily removed from its pot.*

2 *Select a hanging basket with ample drainage (like this cane basket), so that your orchid doesn't get swamped in water. Then place the* Sphagnum *moss or other selected potting mix into the hanging basket.*

Acineta and the large-flowered *Maxillaria sanderiana* and *M. striata* share similar traits to *Stanhopea* and should also be planted using this method.

Many vigorous and rampant growers, which quickly outgrow the confines of a pot due to long rhizomes, can look most impressive when grown in either wooden or wire baskets.

Use stiff wire hangers or decorative chain hangers to hang your baskets. These should be firmly attached to your basket before hanging the plant in your glasshouse. The stiff hangers are certainly easier to hang onto supports from below. You may require a ladder if using the limp chains. A small sturdy hook coming from the pipe or barbed wire with a fishing swivel between the hook and the hanging basket enables the basket to slowly rotate when watering, encouraging even development of pseudobulbs. This is not such an advantage for monopodial orchids or dendrobiums and cattleyas, where you want the plant to concentrate on growing in one direction.

Unlike plants on a bench, plants grown and hung in baskets don't have to compete for light. They also receive plenty of air circulation, which dries the plants out quicker, so keep this in mind when watering. The baskets may be hung at varying heights to utilize the microclimates in the growing area. Baskets placed up high will receive more light and heat, whereas those hung low will be in shadier, cooler, and more humid conditions. Orchids can be placed at varied heights depending on the species and their preferred habitat. Do not be afraid to move plants about until you find the right home for them.

Allow a couple of other plants to grow with the orchids, for example sections of *Tillandsia usneoides* ("Spanish moss," from the bromeliad family) look attractive around wooden baskets. This also helps to increase the humidity around the root zone. However, make sure to water the basket thoroughly, as the dry "moss" will often initially repel water. *Pyrrosia rupestri* ("rock felt-fern") on the outside of *Stanhopea* baskets looks natural and the fern shrivels when dry, so it also acts as a good moisture and humidity indicator. It quickly rehydrates after watering. Invasive sections that interfere with the orchid can easily be removed and either discarded or re-established on the outsides of other baskets.

3 *Before placing the orchid into the hanging basket remove any dead roots, but keep the plant in its original potting medium. Place the orchid into the basket, building up the* Sphagnum *moss around the base of the plant.*

4 *Attach the hook, so the plant may now be hung in the orchid house or from the branch of a shady tree.*

GROWING ORCHIDS ON MOUNTS

In the wild, epiphytic orchid species usually grow on the trunks, branches, or outer twigs of trees. The home-grower will therefore find that many orchids prefer to grow on "slabs" or "mounts" rather than be confined to a plastic pot. In fact, some orchid species will not survive with their roots covered and need to have them exposed to the air.

Many sympodial orchid species have a rambling and often climbing habit, which is difficult to confine to a pot. These plants have long internodes, or elongated rhizomes, between the mature pseudobulbs. They require less maintenance and can be grown undisturbed for many years. Because they are exposed to the air it is impossible to over-water mounted plants as they quickly dry out, which means there is significantly less instance of root rot. The health of the root systems can also be easily monitored. As a bonus, vertically mounted plants take up less room. Also, the pendent growing species are displayed at their best on mounts.

The most popular choices for orchid mounts include treefern slabs, cork (both virgin and compressed), and weathered hardwood (old fence palings). It should be a long-lasting timber, with a bark that will not peel off. There is a range of tree species that can be used successfully, for example, English oak (*Quercus robur*), *Callistemon, Banksia,* and *Hakea.* Sections of she-oaks (*Casuarina*) and paperbark (*Melaleuca*) may also be used, but their timber is particularly susceptible to borer infestation, which reduces the effective life of the host. Pine bark chunks may also be used for smaller epiphytes. Other substrates that have been used with varying degrees of success include inverted terracotta pots, rubber plaques (made from recycled tires), and oasis (moisture-retentive material as used in floral art).

Mount your plants on various species of treefern, either the "soft" treefern (*Dicksonia antarctica*), various species of "hard" treefern (*Cyathea* sp.), or slabs of natural cork

Orchids on mounts

Odontoglossum *hybrid mounted on virgin cork bark. This orchid is mounted on a wire frame which can be hung from the roof of your glass- or shadehouse. Further orchids can be hung from the wire base.*

Bulbophyllum *mounted on treefern fiber. This type of mount would be hung to an A-frame, allowing for air to circulate around the plant.*

(*Quercus suber*). Plastic-coated wire can be used to secure the plants tightly (but not so tight as to sever the rhizome and roots) to the host. Nylon fishing line or strips of pantyhose may also be used. If the plant has few roots (or is a moisture-loving species) include a pad of *Sphagnum* moss around its base. This helps to re-establish many plants with a truncated root system.

Mounted orchids have traditionally been displayed in a vertical manner on the walls of an orchid house or on "A-frames." While this is still very popular, there is a shift to growing species on horizontal slabs. These can be placed directly on the bench with your potted plants or suspended from the roof of your glass- or shadehouse with a wire hook through the center of the mount. Extend the wire under the mount and loop it back onto itself, and then another plant can be hung under this.

Remember that plants grown on slabs require fairly high humidity, ample fresh air circulation, and relatively bright light. Many orchid growers make the mistake of placing their mounted orchids in areas with low humidity and using a watering regime more suited to cacti.

Bulbophyllum *mounted on treefern fiber. Orchids can also be attached to horizontal mounts which can be directly placed on benches next to your potted plants.*

ABOVE
Lemboglossum cordatum *from Central America was previously well known in cultivation as* Odontoglossum cordatum.

LEFT *Place your mounted orchids on "A-frames" within your glass- or shadehouse. This not only saves room, but allows air to circulate around the roots of your orchid.*

REPOTTING

Orchids love being repotted into fresh mix. They seem to get a new lease of life, coupled with a burst of leaf and root growth if the conditions are conducive. Many orchid growers initially assume that repotting should only take place after flowering. This generally applies to late winter or spring flowering orchids, which are about to start their next growth phase. However, experience and observation will tell you that a number of orchids can be "potted-on" at almost any time of the year. This is when an orchid is repotted into a larger pot without disturbing the potting mix. Additional potting mixture is then added to fill the new pot. Orchids can also be divided throughout the year, with the exception of mid-winter and mid-summer when your plants are under particular stress. If the plant is healthy, and the conditions are favorable, there is no reason why your orchid should not flower the following year.

While changes in temperature can influence plant growth, the catalyst that plants respond to most is an increase (or decrease) in day-length. Inspect your plants closely, looking for new growths and fresh root activity, and only repot them if there are visible signs of this active growth. You will find that most orchids in cultivation like to be repotted in spring. Many botanical orchids, which enjoy cooler climates, have their main growth spurt after the heat of summer. They produce most of their growth through autumn and winter. Therefore, these need to be tended to after the hot weather has passed.

Quite simply, orchids need to be repotted when they have outgrown their pots, or the mix has deteriorated. Orchids in *Sphagnum* moss should be repotted at least every two years, athough annually is preferable. Adult cymbidiums like to be repotted every two to three years, with younger plants (seedlings and propagations from back-bulbs) moved annually or even bi-annually. Plants in a bark-based mix can stay in the same pot for up to five years, whereas plants in hanging baskets (in coarse bark) can be content for up to ten years. Sick plants should be repotted into fresh mix or live *Sphagnum* moss regardless of the time of year.

When repotting cattleyas and similar orchids that grow along a straight rhizome, pot the older part of the plant against the rim, with the new growth facing the center of the pot. This will give room for an extra season or two of growth. Make sure all tools are sterilized before you start repotting.

RIGHT *A group of recently repotted* Phalaenopsis *seedlings are already starting to send roots into the fresh bark medium. Young seedlings respond to regular repotting when in active growth.*

Repotting sequence

1 *To repot an orchid, simply squeeze the sides of the plastic pot all of the way around, to loosen the roots that may have attached to the inside of it. This is best done when the potting mix is dry, as the roots slightly contract and make removal easier. Then firmly hold the base of the plant and gently, but firmly, pull the plant out of the pot. Don't be alarmed if you break some of the roots.*

2 *Tease the root system to dislodge most of the spent growing medium, a few rapid shakes from side to side will also assist. Remove any dead roots, either by hand or with secateurs, these will be blackened and often very soft. They are also usually hollow, as seen above.*

3 *Select a larger plastic pot and place a little potting medium at the bottom. Do not fill the pot. You need to leave enough room for the roots of the plant, so that they have room to grow in their new pot.*

4 *Once you have cleaned away all the old potting mix and cut away any dead roots, place the plant toward the center of the new pot. Always sterilize your tools before you move onto a new plant. This prevents the spread of pests and disease.*

5 *Make sure that there's enough room in the new pot for the plant and the roots to grow. Keep the base of the plant level with the top edge of the plastic pot. Hold the plant in the center of the pot and start to fill with new potting mixture.*

6 *Leave the base of the plant level with the top of the potting mix. All of the roots should be covered, with the exception of many vandaceous orchids that will also have aerial roots.*

Compost

Many different media may be used for the cultivation of orchids in pots or baskets. Some may be used exclusively, while others are mixed at various ratios. Whatever compost is used, the main criteria are good aeration and swift drainage. Most orchids cope with their roots being cramped in a pot or container, as long as the compost is open and allows some air to circulate through and around the roots. If you are unsure about the mix you should use for a particular orchid, seek advice from your local orchid nursery. The most common raw materials used for pot culture are listed below and right.

PINE BARK MIX

PINE BARK
Pine bark is readily available in various grades, from very fine, ½ inch (12 mm) to coarse, 1½ inches (38 mm). Composted or treated pine bark (impregnated with small amounts of fertilizer and with most tannins removed) is increasing in popularity as it is suitable for most epiphytic orchid genera. It generally lasts for up to five years. The mix above is a combination of pine bark, perlite, and peat moss.

TREEFERN FIBER
The use of *Osmunda* fiber and treefern fiber was common in epiphytic orchid culture a few decades ago. Generally, treefern is getting harder to obtain because most species are now protected plants. It's used for its moisture holding capabilities, but can quickly become sour if kept wet in warm weather. It is popular in cooler climates.

CHARCOAL
Only good quality chunky grade charcoal, from hardwood trees, should be used as a potting medium. It must be washed beforehand to remove dust and fines. If you want to improve the drainage of your mix this is a good medium to use. However, it should only be used for seedlings or plants that are repotted every couple of years, as charcoal absorbs salts which if left to concentrate will burn the roots. Employ it in combination with other materials, such as pine bark or gravel, with the charcoal component rarely exceeding 20 percent.

GRAVEL

GRAVEL
The use of river gravel or blue-metal adds weight to a mix and assists drainage. It should have a particle size of between ½ to 1 inch (12 to 25 mm). It's usually combined with bark, to about 20 percent of the mix.

SPHAGNUM MOSS MIX

PEAT MOSS MIX

SPHAGNUM MOSS

Sphagnum moss has a very high water-holding capacity and was traditionally used for plants in quarantine, reviving sick dehydrated orchids and striking back-bulbs or back-cuts. Once the plants started growing, they were transferred into a bark-based medium. Today, it is a popular medium used exclusively for a range of orchid genera including some *Bulbophyllum*, *Dendrochilum*, *Dracula*, and *Masdevallia*, particularly mountainous plants that enjoy cooler conditions and year-round moisture. It is still an excellent choice for establishing smaller divisions. Best results are obtained by repotting into fresh moss annually. The mix above is a combination of *Sphagnum* moss, pine bark, and perlite.

PERLITE

This is useful as an additive to orchid composts, and appears as small white particles in the *Sphagnum* and peat moss mixes shown earlier. It is an inert, fine, granular material that "lightens" the mix, while also retaining moisture. Particle size is around ⅛ to ½ inch (4 to 12 mm). It's usually added to horticultural foam, peat, or peat substitute and should be used as 10 percent of the overall potting mixture. It is a popular additive for both epiphytic and terrestrial orchids.

PEAT MOSS

Peat moss varies in quality, but it has high water-retentive qualities. It provides little nutritional value to the plant, but is still an important element of *Cymbidium* composts along with mixes for other terrestrials. The mix above is a combination of peat moss, perlite, and pine bark.

SAND

SAND

Coarse, gritty sand affords excellent drainage, but dries out quickly after watering and has low water-holding capacity. Quartz sands are among the best. Sand is a good additive to terrestrial orchid mixes and is good for *Cymbidium* and other terrestrial genera. Generally, the ratio of its usage varies between 5 to 25 percent of the mix.

PESTS AND DISEASES

The greatest threat to orchids is virus, which affects most popular genera. It weakens the plant and often produces malformed flowers, sometimes with color breaks. The foliage will display a light flecking through both sides of the leaf or a distinct diamond patterning. Unfortunately, there is no cure for infected plants, which should be destroyed. There are many strains that are spread by mites, scales, aphids, plus other sucking and chewing insects.

Using unsterilized cutting implements is the fastest way to spread any type of virus—such as *Cymbidium* mosaic, *Odontoglossum* ring-spot, and orchid fleck virus, a type of rhabdovirus—throughout the orchid collection. Remember, even harvesting your flowers or spent spikes by hand or with cutters may spread a virus. Sterilize your cutting implements by heating to a glow or (after rinsing in water) drenching in bleach or a saturated solution of trisodium phosphate (sugar soap) for five minutes.

Not all insects near your orchids are "bad." Many, such as praying mantids, ladybeetles, and spiders are useful in controlling pests. So, do not kill every creature that you see! However, there are many pests that test the patience of the orchid enthusiast. Caterpillars can make a meal of buds, flowers, and tender new growths if left unchecked. Grasshoppers and crickets can do a lot of damage in a short space of time. *Dendrobium* beetles strip flowers and destroy new growths. Neglected plants will provide homes for sucking insects such as mealy bugs and various species of scale. If plants are kept too dry, red spider mite can become a problem, especially with cymbidiums. Whereas aphids can stunt developing growths and inflorescences.

Frequent hosing under the foliage will help control such invasions. Commercial snail pellets can be laid in damp weather to combat slugs and snails, but must be kept away from young children, birds, and pets. They can be sprinkled on the floor of the orchid house and/or scattered over the plants. Visit your orchid house in the evening, with a flashlight, to catch many nocturnal pests, such as crickets, grasshoppers, and slugs and snails. Either spray the pests or remove and destroy them by hand. Set baited traps if mice and rats are a problem.

The use of insecticide is not advocated (for health reasons and because it can kill "good" insects), and it should only be employed as a last resort. Instead of spraying a whole collection, "spot-spray" for a specific ailment, using a 2-cup (500-ml) atomizer. Two atomizers containing a long-lasting Pyrethum mix are handy to keep in the orchid house for localized application. Check with your local garden center or orchid nursery for advice on what products

GUIDELINES FOR PROPER HYGIENE

Proper hygiene will keep orchids generally free of pests and diseases. Here are some key guidelines:

- *Avoid overcrowding your orchids to ensure they have adequate air circulation.*
- *Regularly remove spent flower spikes and any dead leaves.*
- *Never reuse potting mix.*
- *Sterilize your cutting instruments before moving from plant to plant, whether you are cutting flowers for the vase or repotting and dividing plants.*
- *Be observant, and check for any insects on your plants.*

are registered, recommended, and available for the specific pests in your area. Beware of "spray drift" and only apply in still conditions—preferably first thing in the morning or at sundown. If you have to use pesticides make sure you comply with the manufacturer's instructions, wear protective clothing and a mask, and take a shower afterward. It's important that you follow these rules to prevent contamination.

Fungicides may be used in times of prolonged damp and still conditions to prevent or reduce outbreaks of rot. The best defense against such problems is to have your plants well spaced, to meticulously remove dead leaves and husks from older back-bulbs, and to ensure the plants receive plenty of air circulation. Warm, humid, and still conditions are the ideal breeding grounds for fungal problems.

HEALTHY LEAF

ODONTOGLOSSUM RING SPOT VIRUS

CYMBIDIUM MOSAIC VIRUS

SCALE INSECTS

APHIDS

MEALY BUGS

EARLY SIGNS OF RED SPIDER MITE

SEVERE INFESTATION OF RED SPIDER MITES

PROPAGATION

Propagation is the production or raising of new plants and there are two main methods, vegetative and seed. Vegetative propagation includes division, back cutting, striking back-bulbs, and cuttings. Growing orchids from seed is more complex than simply sowing a bed of annuals in the garden and is usually undertaken in laboratories, where orchid seeds are sown in sterile conditions to avoid contamination by fungi that would otherwise smother the tiny seedlings.

One of the simplest and cheapest ways to increase your orchid collection is to propagate your own plants. Knowing that you can achieve this yourself, without elaborate equipment or techniques, is an added pleasure. A pair of sharp and sturdy secateurs will be all you need for most of these jobs. There are a number of ways that new orchid plants can be reproduced at home.

Division

This is the most common and simplest method of propagating orchids. It should be done with larger plants, preferably at a time coinciding with the start of the plant's main growth cycle in early spring. Most orchids initiate their growth cycles just after the winter equinox. Orchids (and indeed other plants) respond initially to an increase in day length rather than temperature.

Smaller divisions will take longer to re-establish and may not bloom the following season. With paphiopedilums and phragmipediums, it is best not to "cut" the plants to make divisions. They grow and flower better as larger plants. Only separate these if natural divisions fall apart while repotting.

Always use sharp secateurs that have been sterilized in a saturated sugar soap solution made from four tablespoons sugar to 2 cups (500 ml) warm water, or heated to almost glowing. This helps prevent the spread of virus and other unwanted diseases. Remember to sterilize your secateurs or cutting implements before moving on to divide another plant. Follow the steps on the right as a guide to dividing your plant.

Finally, label your plants. Apart from its name, also include the month and year of repotting and any interesting history about the plant (for example, who it came from, price, country of origin or collection data, date of acquisition, and blooming season), depending on the size of the tag. Ultraviolet stabilized tags last a few years, and it's best to push them right into the pot or tie them behind the mount. Fine, permanent black felt markers tend to fade with age, while a lead pencil (about 3B) may not be as esthetically appealing, but is permanent.

Back Cutting

This is a great way to develop specimen plants of the sympodial growth types, such as members of *Cattleya*, *Coelogyne*, *Dendrobium*, *Encyclia,* and *Miltonia*. These plants do not need to be repotted. This method works best with genera that have an exposed rhizome and non-clustering pseudobulbs.

Simply make a full vertical cut halfway between the pseudobulbs, about every three or four growths. This will activate dormant eyes into new growth, often within weeks. This process is best done in late winter or early spring. Again, sterilize your secateurs or cutting implements before moving on to another plant.

1 *First, you need to remove the plant from the plastic pot. Cut down the side of the pot to loosen the plant free.*

2 *Gently peel back the plastic to remove the plant. Look at the growth of the plant and if it's large enough, decide where the divisions will take place. Usually this will involve cutting through the older part of the plant, which may or may not be leafless. If you are not sure at this stage, simply put the plant into a slightly larger pot.*

3 *If you have decided that you are going to divide the plant, make a vertical cut through the rhizome halfway between the pseudobulbs. The cut areas may be dusted with sulfur powder and potted immediately, or may be simply dried for about an hour before potting.*

4 *Cut away the older pseudobulbs, leaving at least four new growths or shoots.*

5 *Tease the root system to dislodge most of the spent growing medium, a few rapid shakes from side to side will also assist. Remove any dead roots, using your hands or secateurs. These will be blackened and often very soft.*

6 *Then simply place the plant toward the center of the new pot and fill with fresh mixture, having the base of the plant level with the top of the potting mix. All of the roots should be covered, with the exception of many vandaceous orchids that will also have aerial roots.*

Back-Bulbs

Genera that can be grown from single back-bulbs include *Calanthe, Catasetum, Coelia, Phaius,* and *Zygopetalum,* and especially *Cymbidium.* Whole potfuls of cymbidiums with dried and leafless back-bulbs look fairly ordinary, even when they are in bloom. The back-bulbs do not benefit the plant except to provide an "insurance policy" in case something happens to the main growing section. When dividing your cymbidiums (and try to keep divisions to at least three pseudobulbs), cut away the back-bulbs individually, remove the dried husks on the bulb, and cut off all the roots.

Each of the back-bulbs should have a dormant "eye" which should shoot if it is healthy. These may be planted in a community pot, or separately, in standard commercially available *Cymbidium* mixture—a free-draining mix created from peat moss and bark chips, or fine bark. Moist *Sphagnum* moss may also be used, as long as you make sure it doesn't stay too wet. Bury the back-bulbs to about a third of the length of the bulb in the mix. Then just treat them as you would your other plants, with perhaps a bit more shade. Keep an eye out for any rot on the bottom half of the bulb, removing and discarding any damaged areas. A new shoot should emerge in three to six months' time if the bulb is back to its full health. It generally takes three or four years for the plants to actually flower, but it is definitely worth the wait for choice cultivars.

There are genera that will only "strike" if there is a cluster of two or three back-bulbs. For these, use a bark-based potting medium or *Sphagnum* moss. They include *Ada, Anguloa, Ansellia, Bifrenaria, Brassia, Bulbophyllum, Cattleya, Coelogyne, Coryanthes, Cuitlauzina, Dendrobium, Dendrochilum, Encyclia, Gongora, Laelia, Lycaste, Maxillaria, Miltonia, Odontoglossum, Oncidium, Osmoglossum, Pholidota, Rhyncholaelia, Rossioglossum,* and *Stanhopea.*

Cuttings

There are a number of vigorous, rambling sympodial orchids (with wandering pseudobulbs that produce aerial roots along the rhizome) that can have small divisions of at least four pseudobulbs removed from them without disturbing the main plant. This is common with small-growing mounted plants or those that climb over the edge of the pot. Genera that may be propagated by this method include *Bulbophyllum, Coelogyne, Dendrobium, Dockrillia, Mediocalcar,* and *Neolauchea.*

Some robust monopodial orchids may also be multiplied by cutting off the top of the plant when it becomes "leggy," as long as there are at least three or four healthy aerial roots to support the severed section. The base of the plant will re-shoot, often in more than one place. This is common practice with many vandaceous-type orchids such as *Aerides, Angraecum, Ascocentrum, Doritis, Jumellea, Sarcochilus* (the lithophytic species), and *Vanda.* This method is also successful for the vine-like habit of *Vanilla.*

RIGHT *A healthy new shoot of a* Cymbidium, *growing from the previous season's pseudobulb.*

FAR RIGHT Stanhopea nigroviolacea *blooms in mid-summer and needs to grow in a basket to allow its pendent flower spears to push through and burst into bloom.*

Aerial Growths

The production of aerial growths is an excellent means of propagation, because it doesn't disturb the parent plant. Aerial growths are produced randomly along sections of pseudobulbs, generally the leafless older sections. Leave these aerials (or "keikis" as they are sometimes known) on the mother plant for at least 12 months. The leaves should have lost their glossy appearance and have their own root system. Often it is best to wait until the aerial produces its first new growth before removal. There is rarely a need to cut them off, as most will easily twist off in your hand. Before cutting off an aerial growth, make sure that it has a healthy, active root system. These young plants, once they have matured, establish very quickly once potted or mounted. Genera with representatives that frequently produce aerial growths include *Dendrobium, Epidendrum, Grastidium,* and *Neobenthamia.* Many *Restrepia* and *Pleurothallis* will also produce young plants from the axis of older leaves.

Aerial Growths

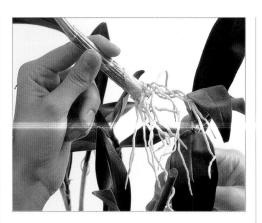

1 *You should not need to cut off the aerial growth, instead, gently twist it off keeping the roots intact.*

2 *Fill a tray with* Sphagnum *moss and sprinkle it with water to provide a damp base for your aerial growths.*

Aerial Bulbs

This is not a common form of natural multiplication, but is frequently employed for *Pleione* species and their hybrids. Small "bulbils," sometimes in clusters, grow from the top of the bulb, in the "crater" left after the leaves have dropped. These may take a few years to flower. They are best removed in late winter, placed in community pots, and treated as seedlings. Sometimes stressed or damaged plants that would not normally multiply this way will produce aerial bulbs as a last attempt to reproduce.

Tuber Division

This method is a recent innovation that has been successfully used to multiply Australian deciduous terrestrial orchids from genera such as *Pterostylis* (greenhoods) and *Diuris* (donkey orchids). The best time to do this is when the plants are in bloom. Firstly, tip the plants out of the pot. At the base of the flowering stem, there will be two tubers. The current tuber, which will be dirty looking, is presently feeding the plant. The new tuber (for next season) will generally be white. Carefully twist off the new tuber, pot it up, and store it in a pot of sand until you repot your other plants after they have become dormant. Then replant the flowering piece (with the old tuber) and keep the pot slightly damp and shaded. Another tuber (or two) may form over the next eight weeks. These will be smaller than the first new tuber and generally take another season to reach flowering size. This is an important way of multiplying rare species and selected clones.

Leaf Cuttings

Most members of the genus *Restrepia* may be proliferated by leaf cuttings, in a similar way to how African violets are struck (but not as quick!). In spring, select a leaf that has flowered (two-year-old leaves seem to work the best) and cut it at the rhizome. Place the "stem" (correctly a ramicaul) into the *Sphagnum* moss, up to the base of the leaf. Be patient as this process can take six months but is a quicker way of duplicating choice (or rare) plants. Up to three new

3 *Place the aerial growths on top of the* Sphagnum *moss, holding the main stem down with a staple or hook.*

4 *You can place more than one aerial growth into each tray, depending on its size. Alternatively, the aerials may also be individually staked and kept in an upright position.*

5 *Although the aerial growths do not look secure, the roots will attach themselves to the potting mix and form a secure root system. They should be repotted when they get too big for the tray.*

plants may develop from healthy leaves. This method has also worked for a few *Pleurothallis* species, generally the single-flowered types that bloom repeatedly from the leaf axil over many months.

Stem Cuttings

This is a productive method used to multiply the terrestrial genus *Thunia*. Do this in the summer, when the plants are in bloom. Firstly, cut off the previous season's leafless cane, about 2½ inches (6 cm) from the base of the plant (don't touch the current leafy growth). Leave the cut piece for a couple of days to seal the wound, then drop it into a tall pot with about 2 inches (5 cm) of *Sphagnum* moss at the bottom. New plants will form over the next few months. It is possible to produce blooming plants within two years by using this method. There are other variations of this method; some involve cutting the stem into sections, while others lay the stem down in a similar way that *Phaius* are propagated.

A similar method works well for dendrobiums. These are hybrids derived from the species *Dendrobium nobile* and its relatives. They produce nodes along the pseudobulbs that, if the growing conditions are correct, will produce blooms in late spring. If the plants are very shaded, receive too much nitrogen fertilizer, or the roots have been damaged, the plant will naturally transform these nodes into young plants at the expense of flowers. However, you can use this knowledge to your advantage. In late spring (when the plants are in bloom), select canes that are at least three years old. It is best to leave three connected growths intact on the main plant. Leave the current growth (with foliage) to bloom next year, any new growth just starting at the base, any flowering growth (remember this process is best done in the blooming season), and last year's growth (which would be leafless, with evidence of flowering last year).

Cut off the old pseudobulbs (three years and older) at the base of the plant. The key here is to find sections of the stem that did not flower. It will appear as a slight bump on the bulb. This will only work on nodes that have not bloomed. Slice into sections halfway between the nodes, leaving two or three nodes between each cut. Discard sections where all the nodes have expired (if they have bloomed, they will not reshoot). Half bury the remaining "stem cuttings" in pots of fine bark, and keep shaded and slightly moist. They will start shooting in about three to six months' time. Leave them in the community pots for two years (obviously discard any sections that rot), and then pot them up individually into 3½ inch (9 cm) pots. These plants will take about three or four years to bloom. If you are keen to multiply a particular clone, you can sacrifice the leading mature growth (that has not flowered), remove the leaves, and follow the above method.

Flower Inflorescences

Some orchids will produce plantlets off spent inflorescences. These include a number of the smaller *Phalaenopsis* species (such as *P. equestris, P. lueddemanniana, P. mariae,* and *P. pallens*), *Sarcochilus ceciliae* and *S. roseus*, many *Epidendrum* species and their hybrids, plus some members of *Oncidium* section *Cyrtochilum* (including *O. falcipetalum, O. serratum,* and *O. superbiens*). The new plantlets develop along dormant eyes either at nodes along the inflorescence or at the end (in the case of the *Sarcochilus*). It takes between one and two years for the plants to be developed enough for removal, so don't take them off prematurely. The application of plant growth hormones, such as keiki paste (a type of acetic acid), can accelerate this process.

Phaius tankervilleae, and the closely related *P. australis* may also be multiplied from the fleshy spent inflorescences. This is best done straight after blooming has ceased. Simply cut the spike off at the base. Along the peduncle (the section of stem before the flowers start), you will notice a few leafy

bracts clasping the stem. Carefully remove these, as they are protecting dormant eyes from which new plants will form. It works best to lay these stems down on seedling trays with either *Sphagnum* moss or a *Cymbidium*-type compost that has a high moisture-retentive content (achieved with the addition of peat moss). Keep them in a shaded and humid situation, and shoots should start to appear within three months. Pot them up individually once they have an active root system. Plants propagated by this method generally take three or four years to bloom.

ABOVE Epidendrum parkinsonianum *is a pendulous growing species from Central America. Its blooms are fragrant in the evening.*

Seed

Orchids produce very fine seed, in very large numbers, that rely on specific fungus or nutrients for germination. Specialist laboratories have the facilities to undertake this seed germination on a commercial scale. The seed is firstly germinated in a sterile agar jelly with a range of nutrients. Upon germination, once the seeds have transformed into manageable protocorms or young plants, they are transferred into flasks that contain a special growth medium for another 12 months or so.

While orchid flasking is out of the scope of many backyard orchidists, you may have success with fresh seed sprinkled on the top of healthy plants, preferably of the same genus. Potted plants with some active root growth around the surface are ideal, as these often harbor the micro-fungi needed to induce germination. If the conditions are conducive, especially with regards to temperature and moisture, you may end up with a few plants. This is how orchids were raised from seed over a century ago, when the first deliberate hybrids were created. The best types of orchids to try growing from fresh seed (to give you practice) are the garden "crucifix orchids" (*Epidendrum radicans* and its hybrids) and many of the Australian temperate dendrobiums, such as *Dendrobium speciosum* and *D. kingianum*.

To pollinate an orchid flower, the pollen needs to be obtained by firstly removing the anther cap with the tip of a toothpick. The pollen (correctly pollinia) will stick to the toothpick and can be transferred directly to the sticky stigmatic surface—located below the anther cap. If the pollination is successful, a fruit (or seed capsule) will form and swell behind the spent bloom. The time taken from pollination to the time the thousands of dust-like seeds are released varies between orchid genera, but can be from six weeks to over twelve months. Orchid seed generally has a short viability, so seed should either be sown immediately or sent off to a seed laboratory within a few weeks. It should be noted that some species are self-incompatible, and therefore require cross pollination, particularly *Angraecum, Dendrobium, Oncidium,* and related genera.

An alternative to growing orchids from seed is to purchase a number of orchid seedlings of a genera you like or are having success with. These can be obtained from most orchid nurseries at a fraction of the cost of adult plants. Most seedlings that are sold can be expected to bloom for the first time in two to five years. For some types, such as *Phalaenopsis,* this can be considerably shorter. The great thing about buying seedlings is that you don't know exactly what you are going to get. Even seedlings from the same crossing can bloom to be quite different, in terms of shape, size, and particularly color.

Tissue Culture

Plants reproduced by mericloning or tissue culture are genetically identical to the parent plant. It is a complex process undertaken in laboratories, where small sections of the meristematic tissue, the actual growing point of the plant, are extracted and multiplied on a medium to proliferate the cells. These are divided and replated into flasks containing an agar growth medium, in a similar mode to seed-raised orchids. The benefit of mericloning has been the production of large numbers of superior cultivars, which are within the budget of most orchid growers. This has been commercially utilized mainly with hybrid cymbidiums, the *Cattleya* alliance, the *Oncidium* alliance, "cut flower" *Dendrobium* hybrids, and some vandaceous orchids. At this stage, the genera *Paphiopedilum* and *Phragmipedium* have proved to be almost impossible to be mericloned as the techniques are not advanced enough. This accounts for the high price of divisions of select cultivars.

ABOVE *A ripe orchid seed capsule.*

BELOW *Professional laboratories use a sterile laminar flow cabinet to sow and replate orchid seed.*

Tissue Culture

A sterilized section of meristematic tissue in agar solution. This is later placed under a florescent lamp, where the temperature is carefully monitored. Within a few days to weeks, the seed will develop into clusters of protocorms.

Within a few months, each protocorm will have produced a tiny leaf from the top and a root from the base.

As the months progress, these plantlets will develop distinguishable leaves (as seen above).

These plantlets are well established with roots, leaves, and small pseudobulbs. They are ready to be removed and potted up.

Part Three

THE ORCHID DIRECTORY

Which orchids does one choose to grow? Before purchasing an orchid for your home, there are a number of factors that need to be considered. Some people prefer pure species, while others are attracted to the more vigorous hybrid combinations. The color of an orchid's bloom may be of prime consideration, as well as the number of times it blooms a year. Whereas fragrant orchids, and there are plenty of them, provide an added bonus to showy blooms. The maximum size of the plant is also an important consideration, especially if space is limited. Rare and unusual orchids are also highly collectable.

The orchids that appear in this fabulous directory demonstrate the diversity within this vast family of plants. Some you may immediately recognize, while others will be much less familiar. Most of them are readily available, and a good-quality orchid nursery will be able to track down special requests, or provide acceptable substitutes. Some of the rarer species may be harder to track down, and may be available only as seedlings.

ANGRAECUM & RELATED GENERA

ANGRAECUM

(from the Malay language angurek, meaning an orchid with a Vanda-like appearance, a monopodial genus having leaves in two ranks) (Pronounced: an-GRAY-cum)

With such a large genus, of over 140 species, there are plants to suit all growers. These monopodial species grow in Madagascar and Africa, and range from warm to cool growing, miniature to large, and clump-forming to rambling plants. In the wild, they frequently grow on rocks and trees, exposed to drying winds and strong light, which accounts for the thick, succulent leaves of many species. Most species have white and green nocturnally perfumed flowers, with a long nectar-filled spur. This scent attracts moths, who play a major role in their pollination. The primary hybrid *Angraecum* Veitchii (*A. sesquipedale* × *A. eburneum*), which is pictured to the right, is a popular and vigorous plant and widely cultivated. The larger growing species need plenty of room to grow, and like a well-drained open medium.

🌡 *Intermediate* ✪ *Semi-shade* 🏵 *Perfumed*

Angraecum compactum is a small growing species from Madagascar with up to 2-inch (50-mm) white blooms. It requires more moisture than its sister species, and does well in small pots of *Sphagnum* moss. If starved of moisture, the leaves will wrinkle and drop off.

🌡 *Cool* ✪ *Shade* 🏵 *Perfumed*

Angraecum didieri is one of the gems of the genus. Also from Madagascar, its 2½-inch (60-mm) pure white summertime blooms often hide the plant. The thick warty roots are silvery white. It will stand the heat of summer, but likes to be kept cool and dry in winter. It grows well in small pots or mounted on tree fern and cork bark.

🌡 *Cool* ✪ *Semi-shade* 🏵 *Perfumed*

Angraecum scottianum is a slender plant with thin stems and semi-terete leaves. Seedlings are quick to mature, and grow well in shaded and moist conditions. This is also a Madagascan species with white flowers 2 inches (50 mm) wide, and a spur up to 6 inches (150 mm) long.

🌡 *Warm* ☀ *Bright* ❀ *Perfumed*

___

Angraecum sesquipadale is
the "King" of this genus. This
Madagascan endemic orchid has
the largest and most spectacular
flowers of the genus. It has up to
four blooms, which open greenish
but turn pure white in a couple
of days. They are up to 8 inches
(200 mm) wide, with a spur up to
11½ inches (300 mm) long. Mature
plants enjoy warm, moist conditions
and strong light.

AERANGIS

(from the Latin, aer = air, angos = vessel, relating to the spur most species have in this genus)
(Pronounced: air-RANG-iss)

This is primarily a genus of about 60 miniature-growing epiphytic
orchids from Madagascar and tropical Africa with disproportionately
large white to cream flowers. These monopodial plants are related to
Angraecum and are one of the genera known as angraecoids. They are
best grown on slabs (either vertical or horizontal), as few like their
roots covered. Larger specimens can be grown in small baskets and
they enjoy strong light and warm conditions. The flowers, with long
nectar-filled spurs, are highly fragrant in the evening. Various species
bloom throughout the year, with the greatest concentration in the
warmer months.

🌡 *Warm* ☀ *Shade* ❀ *Perfumed*

___

Aerangis citrata is unusual, having
up to 30 pale yellow to creamy
white blooms neatly arranged
in two rows. It is endemic to
Madagascar and grows well in
either pots or on slabs.

Aerangis punctata (*left*) is a
distinct species from Madagascar
that has dull gray-green leaves that
are covered in minute silver
dots. Solitary white blooms,
sometimes tinged with green,
are produced in the fall. Vertical
slabs of treefern have proven to
be a very good host for this
disproportionately large
flowered species.

🌡 *Intermediate* ☀ *Shade* ❀ *Perfumed*

🌡 *Warm* ☀ *Semi-shade* ❀ *Perfumed*

___

Aerangis spiculata is one of the
larger growing Madagascan species,
and is a stunning orchid when in
full bloom. The flowers in profile
give the appearance of white birds
in flight. In spring, it produces two-
ranks of pendent sprays with up to
24 white blooms.

AERANTHES

(from the Latin, aer = air, anthos = flower, due to the fact that the flowers appear to be suspended in midair) (pronounced: air-RAN-theez)

This is another primarily Madagascan genus of about 50 angraecoid, monopodial orchids. These epiphytic "Frog Orchids" generally have pendulous wire-like inflorescences, which produce unique green flowers for over a year. Do not be hasty to remove them while they are still green, and only cut them off when they are dead, as they will continue blooming for many months from dormant buds. Their peak flowering season is late winter to summer. They enjoy similar conditions to *Aerangis*, although most species like to have more moisture because of the fine root system. They grow well in suspended pots.

Aeranthes ramosa is one of the most attractive species, available in an array of different forms. Its wire-like inflorescences carry the spidery 3-inch (75-mm), bottle-green flowers that hang below the plant.

🌡 *Intermediate* ✲ *Semi-shade* 🏵 *Perfumed*

BULBOPHYLLUM

(from the Latin, bulbos = bulb, phyllon = leaf, an orchid with a bulb and leaf)
(pronounced: bulb-ow-FY-lum)

This cosmopolitan genus has over 1,000 species with flowers in all shapes, sizes, and colors. New species are still being discovered, with many others not yet formally named by botanists. These sympodial plants grow exclusively as epiphytes and lithophytes. There is a need for a full revision of this diverse genus, as it is inevitable that it will be divided into a number of smaller genera. Some published works have already recognized genera such as *Cirrhopetalum, Hapalochilus,* and *Megaclinium.* However, here, they are included as *Bulbophyllum.*

The majority of species produce a cylindrical pseudobulb with a single leaf, which develops along a creeping rhizome. *Bulbophyllum* includes some of the world's smallest orchids, plus others that form massive plants. The flowers are mostly "un-orchid" like and highly specialized to attract specific pollinators, with highly mobile lips. Most bulbophyllums are creeping plants that only have a short root system, which rarely branches. They prefer shaded conditions and constant moisture around the roots, and grow well on treefern slabs and rafts. Larger species may be grown in shallow saucers, pots, or baskets. Some species of *Bulbophyllum* only flower in response to wet and dry seasons, while others flower throughout the year.

Bulbophyllum carunculatum (*below left*) is an impressive yellowish green -flowered species that blooms in the summer. These blooms are produced on an upright inflorescence, and are up to 4¾ inch (120 mm) long. It is from Sulawesi, and possibly the Philippines. Its robust odor ensures it is fly pollinated.

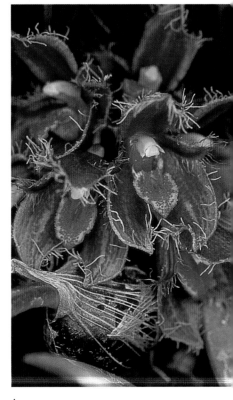

🌡 *Warm* ✹ *Semi-shade*

🌡 *Intermediate* ✹ *Shade*

Bulbophyllum callichroma is a purple-flowered species native to the highlands of New Guinea. It has a creeping habit and grows best on treefern slabs that are kept moist. This method of cultivation allows the long inflorescence of blooms to be best displayed.

🌡 *Warm* ✹ *Bright* ✤ *Perfumed*

Bulbophyllum dayanum (*above*) is an unmistakable species from Myanmar (Burma) and Thailand, with flowers that look like little fuzzy monsters. The blooms are produced in short sprays at the base of the plant, and often have a purple tinge. It grows well on tree-fern slabs and prefers moist, warm conditions in a shaded situation.

🌡 *Intermediate* ✺ *Semi-shade*

Bulbophyllum facetum is a large, single-flowered species, restricted to a small area of montane forest in the Philippines. The brownish-purple mottled flowers of this impressive species open during the morning, before closing late in the afternoon. It grows best in intermediate to warm conditions, and like most bulbophyllums appreciates moist and humid conditions.

🌡 *Warm* ✺ *Bright* ✿ *Perfumed*

Bulbophyllum echinolabium has the largest flowers of the genus, up to 13½ inches (340 mm) from tip to tip. It is endemic to Sulawesi. During the summer, up to four star-shaped blooms are produced sequentially. They are a pink-orange color with a dark purple labellum and short spines. The strong scent is unpleasant during the warmest parts of the day, but it is a small price to pay for the huge, spectacular flowers. It enjoys warm conditions, and its root system should be kept constantly moist.

Warm ✲ *Bright* ✿ *Perfumed*

Bulbophyllum fletcherianum from
New Guinea is one of the largest
growing plants in the genus, and a
member of section *Macrobulbon*. The
plants are imposing, with pendulous,
purple-stained, wide leathery leaves
which can grow up to 40 inches
(1 m) in length. These grow from
pseudobulbs that are often larger
than tennis balls. It has clusters of
up to 20 smooth, but fleshy claret-
colored blooms. These do not
open fully and have a most
unpleasant aroma.

Intermediate ✲ *Semi-shade*

Bulbophyllum frostii is an Indo-
Chinese species that was previously
known as *B. bootanoides*. The blooms
have an unpleasant odor during the
warmer parts of the day, and look a
lot like Dutch clogs in profile.

Bulbophyllum graveolens (*below*) is
a robust tropical species from New
Guinea. It has up to twelve 3-inch
(75-mm) flowers arranged on a
loose umbel. The petals and sepals
are pale green to light orange,
which may or may not be finely
spotted with dark purple. It has a
mobile, bright red labellum. Sadly, it
is another species with a fetid smell.

Warm ✲ *Semi-shade* ✿ *Perfumed*

 *Cool* ✿ *Semi-shade*

Bulbophyllum guttulatum (*above*) is a very pretty species from northern India and Nepal that blooms in late winter. It has a small upright inflorescence with up to eight, greenish-yellow flowers that are finely spotted with purple. The labellum is white with deep pink spots.

Bulbophyllum intersitum is a miniature species from the highlands of New Guinea. Its striped ½-inch (12-mm) tall flowers appear to mimic some of the *Masdevallia* species from South America, even though they are unrelated with vastly different growing habits. It grows quickly if kept cool and moist, preferring treefern slabs as well as small pots of *Sphagnum* moss.

Cool ✿ *Semi-shade*

🌡 *Warm* ☼ *Bright*

Bulbophyllum longiflorum has the widest distribution of the genus, being found in the tropics, from Africa to the Pacific Islands. It produces up to eight blooms that open simultaneously in a semi-circle, and can vary in color from creamy green through golden yellow to deep maroon. It is a vigorous grower when given warm, moist conditions and bright light.

🌡 *Intermediate* ☼ *Shade*

Bulbophyllum leptobulbon is an uncommon single-flowered species from New Guinea, again similar to a *Masdevallia*. It has yellow-green blooms that are produced along the rhizome. These close up slightly in the evening.

🌡 *Warm* ☼ *Bright* ✿ *Perfumed*

Bulbophyllum macrobulbum from New Guinea is another member of section *Macrobulbon*. It has pendulous, purple-stained, wide leathery leaves that can grow close to 40 inches (1 m) in length. Its flowers open widely, and it needs a large growing area to reach its full potential. It likes lots of heat.

Intermediate ✿ *Bright*

Bulbophyllum scaberulum from
southern Africa is a member of
the section *Megaclinium*. Its plant
has two leaves per pseudobulb
and a short, flattened, knife-like
inflorescence with very dark
brownish-purple and yellow
flowers produced either side. These
grow best in hanging baskets in an
open mix of gravel and bark in
moderately strong light.

Cool ✿ *Shade*

Bulbophyllum schillerianum is
a small-flowered Australian
species previously known as
B. aurantiacum. This botanical
orange-flowered taxon, sometimes
called the rope orchid, grows best
on slabs of treefern.

Warm ✿ *Semi-shade*

Bulbophyllum unitubum is an
impressive, large single-flowered
species from New Guinea. It enjoys
warm, moist conditions and can
bloom a number of times during
the year.

🌡 *Warm* ☸ *Semi-shade*

***Bulbophyllum* Daisy Chain** is
an aptly named hybrid between
B. makoyanum and *B. amesianum*. It
grows best on slabs, and tends to
bloom throughout the year, with
the best flowerings occuring in
the warmer months.

***Bulbophyllum* Elizabeth Ann
'Buckleberry'** is a hybrid between
the large-flowered *B. longissimum*
and *B. rothschildianum*. Both of
these species are members of
the *Cirrhopetalum* section of
Bulbophyllum. This section has
distinctive flowers which are
produced in an umbel, with lateral
(lower) sepals that are fused, and
filaments and appendages on the
dorsal (upper) sepal and petals.
These "flags" move in the slightest
breeze and help attract pollinators.
This award-winning hybrid is easily
grown in a range of temperatures.

🌡 *Intermediate* ☸ *Bright*

CATTLEYA & RELATED GENERA

CATTLEYA
(after William Cattle, a nineteenth century, English orchid enthusiast)
(pronounced: KAT-lee-yah)

The genus *Cattleya*, from tropical America, is one of the most popular groups of orchids in cultivation, with over 50 species. These sympodial rock and tree dwellers have showy, long-lasting, and often highly fragrant flowers produced on stout plants with club-shaped to cylindrical pseudobulbs. They are topped with one (unifoliate) or two (bifoliate) dull green leathery leaves. Most species require warmth in winter, however the Brazilian bifoliate fall-flowering types will stand cooler temperatures for short periods, as long as they are kept dry during their dormant phase. They require good drainage and a coarse bark-based medium. Healthy plants will develop an extensive system of thick white roots, which are long-lasting and branch freely. There have been thousands of hybrids made within the genus and related members of the *Cattleya* alliance, especially *Laelia*, *Rhyncholaelia* (often credited in the hybrid lists under *Brassavola*), and *Sophronitis*, with many of the larger flowering types grown commercially for cut flower production. They are popular indoor plants, happy on bright window ledges with strong light. *Cattleya* are susceptible to mealy bugs and scale insects that can hide behind the papery sheaths of the pseudobulbs and behind the blooms.

🌡 *Cool* ✲ *Bright* ✿ *Perfumed*

Cattleya × ***venosa*** is a natural hybrid between the species *C. forbesii* and *C. harrisoniana,* and is native to Brazil. It is a fine garden plant when in frost-free zones, and is also an ideal candidate for a sunny window ledge, as it is free-flowering and has a compact growing plant.

Cattleya **Earl 'Imperialis'** is a popular florist's flower because of its large, crisp white blooms. It was bred from the albino forms of *C. trianaei, C. gaskelliana,* and *C. mossiae.*

🌡 *Intermediate* ✲ *Bright* ✿ *Perfumed*

🌡 *Intermediate* ✿ *Bright* ✿ *Perfumed*

Cattleya Eclipse is a primary hybrid between *C. maxima* and *C. skinneri*, producing clusters of large magenta flowers in spring.

Cattleya Miyuki is a floriferous hybrid that quickly grows to specimen size. It produces numerous sprays of

beautiful, bicolored hot pink and bright, yellow-throated showy blooms.

🌡 *Cool* ✿ *Bright* ✿ *Perfumed*

🌡 *Intermediate* ✹ *Bright* 🏵 *Perfumed*

Cattleya **Margaret Degenhardt 'Saturn'** is one of the splash-petaled types, bred from the peloric *C. intermedia* var. *aquinii*. The other parent is *C.* Bob Betts. This hybrid can often bloom twice a year.

🌡 *Cool* ✹ *Bright* 🏵 *Perfumed*

Cattleya **Hallie Rogers 'Amy'** is a compact growing hybrid that produces a bold display of blooms twice a year from a small plant. This is due to the influence in its background of *C. walkeriana*, that is itself a small growing species.

Cattleya **Luteous Forb** is a primary hybrid between the species *C. luteola* and *C. forbesii*, producing clusters of apple flowers off compact plants. These can bloom more than once a year.

🌡 *Intermediate* ✹ *Bright* 🏵 *Perfumed*

BRASSAVOLA

(after A.M. Brassavole, an Italian botanist) (pronounced: bra-SAH-vol-la)

This is a genus of about 30 terete-leafed epiphytic orchids from Central and South America. They are interesting plants even when not in bloom. The plants are often pendant shaped and produce impressive displays of white to pale green clusters of flowers, which are fragrant in the evening. They grow well in small pots, baskets, or slabs, as long as they dry out between waterings. They enjoy high light, intermediate to warm temperatures, and can take cool temperatures in winter if kept dry. They have been used in a number of novelty hybrids (orchids with bright and unsual colors and a distinctive shape) with related genera.

Brassavola cucullata *(below, left)* from Central America has a pendulous growth habit, which makes it an ideal candidate for slab culture. The individual flowers are quite large, and lax, with yellow-green segments and a white labellum that is partially serrated.

Intermediate ✿ *Bright* ❀ *Perfumed*

Brassavola nodosa is a variable species found over a wide range of countries. It is known as the "Lady of the Night," because of its highly scented blooms. Flower color is white, through cream to pale green, with fine purple spotting at the base of the labellum. It grows quickly if given humid conditions, coupled with high temperatures and bright light.

Intermediate ✿ *Bright* ❀ *Perfumed*

BROUGHTONIA
(after Arthur Broughton, an English botanist) (pronounced: braw-TOE-nee-ah)

This is a genus of only two miniature, warm-growing, epiphytic species (*B. negrilensis* and *B. sanguinea*) from Jamaica in the West Indies. There have been numerous artificial hybrids combining *Broughtonia* with members of the related *Laeliinae*, including *Cattleytonia* (× *Cattleya*), *Laeliocatonia* (× *Cattleya* × *Laelia*), Laelonia (× *Laelia*), and *Otaara* (× *Brassavola* × *Cattleya* × *Laelia*). These have produced compact plants, with upright sprays of shapely flowers in a wide range of colors.

🌡 *Warm* ☀ *Bright*

Broughtonia sanguinea is endemic to Jamaica. It comes in an array of colors, ranging from pale pink to red-purple, white, and yellow. In addition, some attractive bi-colored and splash-petaled forms have been developed by selective breeding. Up to 12 round and flat, 1½-inch (38-mm) blooms are produced on long inflorescences. They grow well on cork slabs, with the plants requiring strong light. It has been extensively propagated from seed, with the resulting seedlings being much easier to cultivate than wild collected plants.

LAELIA

(after Laelia, one of the Vestal Virgins) (pronounced: LAY-lee-ah)

The genus *Laelia*, with about 70 members from tropical South America, is a very fashionable group of easily grown, showy, and colorful orchids. Most are lithophytic, although there are also a number of epiphytic species. They differ from *Cattleya* by having eight pollinia (*Cattleya* only have four). On the whole they are unifoliate, but there are a few species with two leaves. Most species require bright, warm, and moist conditions during summer, while the plants are in active growth, and a cooler, dry winter, when most species are dormant. Cultivated plants must have unimpeded drainage, and can be mounted or grown in pots using a coarse bark-based medium.

Laelia anceps is an extremely variable, in both plant height and flower color, fall to winter blooming species from Mexico, with large, star-flowered, 4¼-inch (110-mm) flowers. Up to five blooms can be produced, off long, flattened inflorescences that can be up to 40 inches (1 m) long. The color ranges from white, through various shades of pink to deep lavender. The labellum color is equally variable, with possible combinations of white, yellow, orange, purple, and lilac. Also in cultivation is the albino (for example, *Laelia anceps* var. *alba* 'Jannine'), bi-colored and splash-petalled forms (for example, *Laelia anceps* 'Brooke').

🌡 *Cool* ☀ *Bright*

🌡 *Cool* ☀ *Bright*

🌡 *Cool* ☀ *Bright*

Intermediate ✺ *Bright* ✾ *Perfumed*

Intermediate ✺ *Bright* ✾ *Perfumed*

Laelia crispa (*above*) is a Brazilian species that looks like one of the larger *Cattleya* species. It can produce up to seven white blooms, with a contrasting labellum that has a network of deep purple venation.

Laelia flava (*below*) is a compact, rock-growing plant with tall, erect spikes of yellow flowers in spring and early summer. The fifty 2-inch (50-mm) blooms cluster at the top of the scape. It is native to Brazil.

Intermediate ✺ *Bright*

Laelia purpurata is the national flower of Brazil, and has been called the "Queen of the Laelias." Up to five, 8-inch (200-mm) blooms are produced from the mature pseudobulbs each summer. It is tall-growing, in a wide range and combination of colors, from pure white, through all the shades of pink, purple, and lilac. The flared and trumpet-like labellum has a similar color range, with a network of stripes and solid color. There are albino (pure white), semi-alba, splash-petaled, and bi-colored forms. There have been numerous varieties named, all defining a different color form. Two of the most popular are *Laelia purpurata* var. *carnea* (white, with a soft pink labellum) and *L. purpurata* var. *werkhauseri* (white, with a dark bluish-purple labellum). This species also has a delightful perfume.

SCHOMBURGKIA

(after Sir Richard Schomburgk, a German botanist) (pronounced: shom-BURK-ee-ah)

This is a small genus with about 12 species that resemble some of the larger *Laelia* species, to which they are closely related. Growing conditions are the same as for cattleyas and laelias, however these robust orchids demand higher light levels to flower well. Although, some species can be grown in full sun in the tropics, most appreciate protection from the heat of midsummer with some light shading. Their rambling growth makes them difficult to contain in pots, and often they will only bloom once they are either pot bound or have grown out of their pots via the elongated rhizome.

Schomburgkia superbiens is from Central America, and has been classified previously as both a *Cattleya* and *Laelia*. The inflorescence can grow over 40 inches (1 m) tall on healthy specimens, with large mauve flowers produced in the fall. *Schomburgkia superbiens* var. *alba* (left) is a very rare albino color form that is much prized in cultivation.

 Intermediate ✳ *Bright*

SOPHRONITIS

(from the Latin, sophros = modest, relating to the small stature of the plant)
(pronounced: soff-RON-eye-tiss)

This is a small genus of about eight brightly colored epiphytic orchids from Brazil and Bolivia. They are closely related to the genus *Laelia*, in particular the section *Hadrolaelia*, which includes species such as *L. dayana* and *L. pumila*. These laelias and *Sophronitis* share similarities in having single, colorful blooms, and an inflorescence without a sheath, with the young leaf folding around the buds. As a group, they are best grown in cool to intermediate conditions. They prefer to grow in pots, with a *Sphagnum* moss based mix for the smaller plants and a bark-based mix for larger ones. They need to be repotted every two years, as they will quickly lose their roots in a stale medium. Keep them in a humid environment with medium light levels, and reduce the amount of watering in winter. *Sophronitis* have been used in hybrids within the *Cattleya* alliance, creating compact plants with bright, shapely blooms.

Sophronitis coccinea is a magnificent species from southern Brazil. It has large, 3-inch (75-mm), round, flat blooms that range from bright orange to scarlet-red. The labellum is very narrow, often with yellow and orange markings. There is also an "albinistic" form with yellow flowers. It likes a lot of fresh air, and does not tolerate stagnant conditions. There is continual line breeding of this showy species, which display more improved vigor than wild specimens. Unfortunately, it will not thrive in tropical, lowland conditions, however *S. cernua* would be a suitable candidate for warmer environments. *S. grandiflora* is a synonym.

 Cool ✺ *Semi-shade*

BRASSOLAELIOCATTLEYA

(a tri-generic hybrid involving Brassavola, Laelia, and Cattleya) (pronounced: bra-SOW-lay-lee-oh-KAT-lee-yah)

Many of the hybrids listed as involving *Brassavola* invariably have *Rhyncholaelia digbyana*, then known as *Brassavola digbyana*, as one of the parents. *Rhyncholaelia digbyana* is the national flower of Honduras. It has stunning, very large, up to 6-inch (150-mm), green flowers. The labellum is lighter green and white, and is deeply fimbriated or fringed. These durable plants have a growth habit that's very similar to the unifoliate cattleyas. The foliage has a bluish green appearance. These hybrids require warmth in winter, but will stand cooler temperatures for short periods, as long as they are kept dry during their dormant phase. They must have unimpeded drainage and a coarse bark-based medium. Healthy plants will develop an extensive system of thick white roots, which are long-lasting and branch freely. Many of the larger flowering types are grown commercially for cut flower production. They are popular plants for indoors, enjoying a bright window ledge with strong light needed by day to keep the plants healthy.

🌡 *Intermediate* ✦ *Bright* ✿ *Perfumed*

Brassolaeliocattleya Dundas 'Olga' is a classic example of one of the finest cultivars in purple cattleyas. It produces up to three large flowers that are highly fragrant and last for many weeks.

🌡 *Intermediate* ✦ *Bright* ✿ *Perfumed*

Brassolaeliocattleya Alma Kee 'Tipmalee' has a large genetic influence from the warm-growing species, *Cattleya dowiana* var. *aurea*. The color contrast between the bright yellow petals and sepals to the bright red labellum is striking.

🌡 *Intermediate* ✦ *Bright* ✿ *Perfumed*

Brassolaeliocattleya Mount Sylvan 'Susan' is heavily influenced by *Cattleya mossiae* and has a sweet fragrance. This hybrid grex has won many awards and prizes at orchid shows.

***Brassolaeliocattleya* Waianae
Leopard** is a cluster-type hybrid
that is heavily influenced by the
spotted *Cattleya guttata*.

***Brassolaeliocattleya* Williette
Wong** is named after the wife of a
past president of the Honolulu
Orchid Society. This is another
eye-catching plant that gets its
distinctive color from *Cattleya
dowiana* var. *aurea*.

***Brassolaeliocattleya* Pokai
Tangerine 'Lea'** is a colorful
hybrid with glossy flowers. It was
created in Hawaii, with the orange
species *Cattleya aurantiaca* in its
background.

CATTLEYTONIA

(a bi-generic hybrid between Cattleya and Broughtonia) (pronounced: KAT-lee-tone-ee-yah)

Cattleytonia is a genus created by combining members of *Cattleya* with *Broughtonia*. These are often highly colored hybrids with flowers produced on tall, thin but sturdy inflorescences off compact plants. Cultivation is similar to that applied for *Cattleya*, except that the plants do not tolerate the cold, and prefer intermediate to warm conditions year round. They must have unimpeded drainage and a coarse bark-based medium. They are popular plants for indoor culture, as they are small and compact and come in a range of bold colors, from reds and purples to yellows and whites. Cattleytonias enjoy a bright window ledge with about six hours of strong light needed per day to keep the plants healthy.

Cattleytonia **Why Not 'Roundabout'** is arguably the most popular hybrid in the genus on account of its ease of culture and fire engine red blooms. It is the result from the primary hybrid between the species *Cattleya aurantiaca* and *Broughtonia sanguinea*.

🌡 *Warm* ☀ *Bright*

DIALAELIA

(a bi-generic hybrid between Diacrium [now Caularthron] and Laelia)
(pronounced: die-ah-LAY-lee-ah)

This is a warm growing genus, and is a hybrid between *Caularthron* and *Laelia*. *Caularthron bicornutum* was previously known as *Diacrium bicornutum*. *Dialaelia* require intermediate to warm conditions throughout the year. They must have unimpeded drainage and a coarse bark-based medium. As with cattleytonias, they are popular plants for indoor culture because of their small, compact size and range of bold colors, from reds and purples to yellows and whites. They enjoy a bright window ledge with about six hours of strong light needed per day.

Dialaelia **Snowflake 'Frosty'** is a warm growing hybrid between *Caularthron bicornutum,* from Central America and the West Indies, and *Laelia albida* from Mexico. It can bloom more than once a year, usually in the spring and summer. Keep the plant warm and dry during winter.

🌡 *Warm* ✸ *Bright* ✿ *Perfumed*

LAELIOCATTLEYA

(a bi-generic hybrid between Laelia and Cattleya) (pronounced: Lay-lee-oh-KAT-lee-yah)

This group comprises a wide range of colorful hybrids between members of the genera *Cattleya* and *Laelia*. These hybrids do not include any representatives from other related genera. They are generally robust plants with one or two leaves, but require warmth in winter. However they will withstand cooler temperatures for short periods, as long as they are kept dry during their dormant phase. They must have unimpeded drainage and a coarse bark-based medium. Healthy plants will develop an extensive system of thick white roots, which are long-lasting and branch freely. Many of the larger flowering types are grown commercially for cut flower production and are often used in corsages. They are popular plants for indoor culture, enjoying a bright window ledge with about six hours of strong light needed per day to keep them healthy. Watch out for mealy bugs and scale insects that can hide behind the papery sheaths of the pseudobulbs and behind the blooms. These can be controlled with pyrethrum spray or a recommended insecticide.

Laeliocattleya **Burgundy Gem 'Jannine'** *(left)* is a small, compact hybrid with large velvet-like purple flowers that are influenced by its parent *Laelia pumila*.

🌡 *Intermediate* ☀ *Bright*

🌡 *Intermediate* ☀ *Bright*

Laeliocattleya **C G Roebling 'Coerulea'** is a very old primary hybrid made over a century ago, between the "blue-lipped" forms of *Cattleya gaskelliana* and *Laelia purpurata*.

Intermediate ✲ *Bright* ✿ *Perfumed*

Laeliocattleya **Edgard Van Belle 'Hausermann'** is a bold purple bloom that has a strong fragrance.

Intermediate ✲ *Bright*

Laeliocattleya **Tangerine Dream 'Lynette'** is an example of the style of hybrid known as "Cocktail Cattleyas" that are characterized by their bunches of bright orange blooms, an influence from *Cattleya aurantiaca*.

Cool ✲ *Bright*

Laeliocattleya **Mini Purple 'Coerulea'** has blue-lilac flowers, and is a primary hybrid between *Laelia pumila* and *Cattleya walkeriana*.

Intermediate ✲ *Bright* ✿ *Perfumed*

Laeliocattleya **Tropical Pointer 'Cheetah'** is a *Cattleya intermedia* hybrid that gets its spots from one of its ancestors, *Cattleya aclandiae*.

POTINARA

(a multi-generic hybrid involving Brassavola, Cattleya, Laelia, and Sophronitis—named after French orchid grower Monsieur Potin) (pronounced: POT-in-ar-rah)

Potinara has four different genera in its genetic makeup, being a combination of *Brassavola, Cattleya, Laelia,* and *Sophronitis*. Potinaras are very similar to sophrolaeliocattleyas but differ in having an extra infusion of *Brassavola*. Generally, the flowers are also slightly larger. Potinarias enjoy intermediate to warm conditions throughout the year, and must have unimpeded drainage and a coarse bark-based medium. They are popular plants for indoor culture because they are small, compact, and come in a range of bold colors, from reds and purples to yellows and whites. They enjoy a bright window ledge, with about six hours of strong light needed per day to keep the plants healthy.

🌡 *Intermediate* ✹ *Bright* ✿ *Perfumed*

***Potinara* Burana Beauty** is a distinctive two-tone splash-petaled hybrid. The markings on the labellum are also expressed in the petals. Cultivars such as this are often multiplied by mericloning or tissue culture.

🌡 *Intermediate* ✹ *Bright*

***Potinara* Aussie Spirit 'Rebekah'** *(above)* is a free-flowering hybrid. It is most complex, with over 16 different species in its background.

***Potinara* Free Spirit 'Louanne'** *(left)* is an outstanding hybrid on account of its shape and clear, bold color. Its shape is influenced by *Sophronitis coccinea* with the color coming from *Cattleya luteola*.

🌡 *Intermediate* ✹ *Bright*

🌡 *Intermediate* ✹ *Bright*

***Potinara* Haw Yuan Gold 'DJ'** was a Taiwanese bred hybrid that was the Grand Champion at the 16th World Orchid Conference in Vancouver, Canada in 1999. Its intense golden color and large size are the primary reasons this plant has won many major awards and championships.

SOPHROLAELIOCATTLEYA

(a tri-generic hybrid involving Sophronitis, Laelia, and Cattleya)
(pronounced: soff-ROW-lay-lee-oh-KAT-lee-yah)

Sophrolaeliocattleya is a three-way hybrid combining *Sophronitis*, *Laelia*, and *Cattleya*. Most of these hybrids have the cool growing *Sophronitis coccinea* in their background. The introduction of this species creates smaller growing plants, and strong red colored flowers that have a more defined shape. The yellow-flowered hybrids often have *Cattleya luteola* in their lineage. All of these orchids enjoy typical *Cattleya* conditions, but prefer extra shading and slightly cooler temperatures.

Intermediate ☀ *Bright*

***Sophrolaeliocattleya* Jungle Beau 'Jannine'** is a very colorful hybrid bred from *Sophrocattleya* Beaufort (*Sophronitis coccinea* × *Cattleya luteola*).

Intermediate ☀ *Bright* ❀ *Perfumed*

***Sophrolaeliocattleya* Hazel Boyd 'Apricot Glow'** is a very popular clone of this successful American-bred hybrid, between *Sophrolaeliocattleya* California Apricot and *Sophrolaeliocattleya* Jewel Box.

Intermediate ☀ *Bright* ❀ *Perfumed*

***Sophrolaeliocattleya* Hazel Boyd 'Redstone'** is another example of this hybrid, this time in the red tones.

Intermediate ☀ *Bright*

***Sophrolaeliocattleya* Seagulls Mini-Cat Heaven 'Jannine'** is a small plant with a very long name. This style of hybrid blooms readily from young plants, and they like to be kept in small pots.

COELOGYNE & RELATED GENERA

COELOGYNE

(from the Latin koilos, referring to the cavity on the column) (pronounced: SEE-lodge-en-nee)

Coelogyne is a large diverse group of about 200 sympodial orchids of Asian origin. Most of the members of this showy genus of epiphytes and lithophytes have white or green flowers, with contrasting labellums displaying many brown markings. Coelogynes are generally plants from mountainous regions, and about 80 percent of the species are suitable for cultivating in cool to intermediate conditions. However there are also species from the monsoonal, tropical lowlands which are generally very easy to grow and will rapidly build into specimen plants if the conditions are favorable. Most species are grown in pots with a bark-based mix, however those with pendulous flower spikes, or rampant growers with long rhizomes, are best accommodated in baskets. As a bonus, several species have pleasantly fragrant blooms. There have been a number of hybrids registered; some of the best include *C.* Jannine Banks (*flaccida* × *mooreana*), *C.* Linda Buckley (*mooreana* × *cristata*), and *C.* Unchained Melody (*cristata* × *flaccida*). *Coelogyne* are related to *Dendrochilum, Pholidota,* and *Pleione.*

🌡 *Cool* ✪ *Shade*

Coelogyne mooreana is a rare, cool growing species from Vietnam, and is arguably the queen of the genus. Up to eight large and well shaped, glistening, 3½-inch (90-mm), white flowers are produced on erect to arching inflorescences in spring and summer.

Coelogyne cristata *(left)* is a cool-growing Himalayan species and is, arguably, the most popular species in cultivation. Lovely sprays of up to eight crystalline white, fragrant, undulating flowers, with orange markings on the labellum are produced in early spring. *Coelogyne cristata* var. *lemoniana* has yellow markings on the labellum, while *C. cristata* var. *hololeuca* is the albino form.

🌡 *Cool* ✪ *Semi-shade*

🌡 *Cool* ✺ *Semi-shade*

Coelogyne **Jannine Banks 'Snow White'** is an outstanding horticultural hybrid between *C. flaccida* and *C. mooreana*. It has up to 12 white to cream blooms with a contrasting orange and brown marked labellum. Flowering occurs more than once a year, with flushes from winter to early summer.

🌡 *Cool* ✺ *Shade*

Coelogyne punctulata has a wide distribution from Nepal across to southern China. It can often be labeled incorrectly as *C. nitida*, which is a distinct species. *Coelogyne punctulata* appreciates cool, moist conditions to grow to its full potential.

🌡 *Cool* ✺ *Semi-shade*

Coelogyne **Linda Buckley** is a popular hybrid between the white-flowered species *C. cristata* and *C. mooreana*. Its wavy blooms appear in late winter to early spring. It prefers cool conditions.

DENDROCHILUM

(from the Latin dendron = tree, and cheilos = lip, an obscure reference to the epiphytic growth habit) (pronounced: den-dro-KYE-lum)

Members of this large genus of 300 botanicals are sympodial, with a single leaf. The majority are epiphytes that grow in the cloud forests of mountainous regions, where there are rarely significant temperature fluctuations. Only a few species make their homes in the tropical lowlands. They bloom once a year, with the developing new growth, and their small but often colorful flowers are arranged alternately along an inflorescence that is spiraled in some species. The center of distribution for the genus *Dendrochilum* is the Philippines, with numerous species in Borneo and Sumatra. Dendrochilums in the main are very easy to grow. Most are clump forming, and look most attractive when grown in pots. Use *Sphagnum* moss solely as a medium for the miniature growers, and any plants up to 4 inches (100 mm) in pot size. Larger plants go into a bark-based mix, with the addition of a small proportion of gravel, perlite, and chopped moss. Fresh air and constant high humidity is most important, and they will happily bloom in shaded conditions. Try to keep the plants as cool as possible during hot summer months, but protect them from the chill of winter.

🌡 *Cool* ☀ *Shade*

Dendrochilum stenophyllum is from the Philippines and has thin-textured, upright green leaves, with the plant growing in clumps. The arching inflorescences appear with the new growth, in late winter, and carry up to 30 white to cream, tiny flowers. The overall floral display is quite impressive.

🌡 *Intermediate* ☀ *Semi-shade*

Dendrochilum longifolium is a variable species that is common in New Guinea, but also occurs in Indonesia, Malaysia, and parts of the Philippines. The inflorescence is longer than the leaves and bears up to forty, ½-inch (12-mm) green blooms. The labellum is the same color, but with two brown stripes. This species has a strong spicy fragrance and generally flowers in late summer, however different individuals of the same species will bloom at other times.

🌡 *Cool* ☀ *Shade*

Dendrochilum tenellum is a common species found throughout the Philippine archipelago, often forming large clumps on moss covered rainforest trees. It has tiny white to dirty cream flowers in late winter to early spring. It is one of the most "unorchid-like" species in foliage, with very fine terete grass-like leaves. A well-grown plant can be likened to the filament lamps, which were in vogue years ago.

🌡 *Intermediate* ✳ *Shade*

Dendrochilum wenzelii has stiff, dark-green, narrow, and channeled leaves. The flowers are unusual for the genus in being dark red in their normal form, even though there are rare forms with brown, orange, or yellow blooms. The inflorescence appears with the new growth, in late winter, and carries up to thirty ½-inch (12-mm) flowers that open fully. This distinct and fast growing species is also endemic to the Philippines.

PLEIONE

(from the Greek pleione = annual, referring to the short-lived leaves of members of the genus)
(pronounced: plee-OW-nee)

This is a small genus of mostly semi-alpine, bulbous orchids from Nepal to China. They are terrestrials and epiphytes, and prefer the high altitude of mountainous habitats, growing on mossy limbs or fallen rotten logs. Their showy *Cattleya*-like blooms appear in spring, and are produced singly or in pairs. Pleiones are easy to cultivate in cool situations and perform at their best if repotted annually, in a rich, well-drained terrestrial mix. The pseudobulbs are best planted (not buried), as groups, in squat pots, saucers, or trays, as they have a shallow root system. Healthy plants produce two new growths, which develop into new plants, as the older pseudobulbs shrivel and die. Keep the potting mix moist from spring to early fall, while the plants are actively growing. They need to be cool and dry during the winter. There have been numerous hybrids made using *P. formosana* as a foundation and incorporating some of the more difficult to grow, yellow-flowered species from China. The more vigorous and popular hybrids include *Pleione* Alishan, *Pleione* Erebus, *Pleione* Piton, *Pleione* Shantung, and *Pleione* Versailles.

🌡 *Cool* ✳ *Shade*

Pleione formosana is from east China and Taiwan, and is the hardiest species in the genus. The 4-inch (100-mm) flowers come in numerous shades of pink (with many named cultivars), but there are also pure white forms. The fringed labellum has a white and yellow base, with small, red-brown blotches. *Pleione formosana* var. *alba* 'Snow White' (above) is a popular albino form of the species.

Pleione **Erebus 'Redshank'** *(left)* is named after an active volcano in Antarctica, and has striking color in the labellum.

🌡 *Cool* ✹ *Shade*

🌡 *Cool* ✹ *Shade*

Pleione **Piton** is a musk pink hybrid that has taller stems than most cultivars.

🌡 *Cool* ✹ *Shade*

Pleione **Shantung 'David Harberd'** is one of the hybrids bred from the yellow *Pleione forrestii*, which accounts for its unusual color.

CYMBIDIUM

(from the Greek kymbos = boat, referring to the boat-shaped labellum)
(pronounced: sim-BID-ee-um)

The genus *Cymbidium* has some 50 or so species, distributed throughout Asia and Australia. Most are terrestrial, with upright to arching flower spikes, bearing blooms in many colors. In the lowlands, cymbidiums take to the trees, growing in high light. Many have long pendent inflorescences and thick leathery leaves. China and Japan have cultivated these orchids for centuries, where they are valued for spiritual and medicinal purposes. Variegated leafed and unusual flower forms are also highly prized. Most hybrid cymbidiums are grown in commercially available orchid compost, which is free draining but retains some moisture. Fine grade pine bark produces excellent results. The epiphytic species prefer a mix incorporating a high percentage of coarse bark. In the main, they like to be kept moist year-round, with increased watering and fertilizing from spring to fall, while they are in active growth. Tens of thousands of hybrids have been artificially created over the past century, which are often loosely categorized by their flower size. These classifications range from miniature, ¼ inch (6 mm), intermediate, ½ to 4 inches (12 to 100 mm), and standard, over 4 inches (100 mm). Traditionally, the main flowering season has been winter to spring, however selective breeding is extending this. Most of the cool-growing species and complex hybrids need a nighttime drop in temperature of at least 18°F (10°C) during summer, to help initiate flowering for the following season. This can be manipulated by giving the plants a regular misting of water at sundown during warm months.

🌡 *Cool* ✲ *Bright* ✿ *Perfumed*

Cymbidium lowianum is a hardy terrestrial species—distributed from Myanmar (Burma), through Thailand to southern China. It has very long arching spikes, of up to thirty, 3½-inch (90 mm) olive green flowers, with a contrasting cream and red lip.

Cymbidium erythrostylum is endemic to Vietnam and blooms in the fall. It has up to ten, 2½-inch (60-mm) white flowers with a labellum displaying a network of thick red-orange veins over a yellow and white base. The petals do not open fully and tend to embrace the column and lip.

🌡 *Cool* ✲ *Bright* ✿ *Perfumed*

🌡 *Cool* ✲ *Bright* ✿ *Perfumed*

Cymbidium lowianum var. *concolor* is the albino form of the species that has been used to create many of the green hybrids.

🌡 *Cool* ✤ *Bright* ✤ *Perfumed*

Cymbidium tracyanum is a large cool-growing species, from northern Myanmar (Burma), Thailand, and southern China. It has strongly fragrant, 5½-inch (140-mm) flowers that are olive green, heavily marked, and striped with red-brown, giving the bloom an overall deep bronze appearance.

🌡 *Cool* ✤ *Bright*

Cymbidium Autumn Crisp 'Cinnabar' is one of the compact standard hybrids that have round flowers in the fall with sunset tones.

🌡 *Intermediate* ✤ *Bright* ✤ *Perfumed*

Cymbidium Australian Midnight 'Tinonee' is a robust plant that prefers warmer conditions and stronger light than most cymbidiums. Its deep claret blooms are almost black. This is a primary hybrid between the epiphytic species *C. canaliculatum* and *C. atropurpureum*.

🌡 *Cool* ✤ *Bright* ✤ *Perfumed*

Cymbidium Viva Las Vegas 'Royale' highlights some of the newer colors being developed in the modern standard hybrids.

🌡 *Cool* ❂ *Bright* ❀ *Perfumed*

***Cymbidium* Devon Gala 'Geyserland'** *(above)* is a miniature orchid with an almost black and white flower, a legacy from the *C. devonianum* influence.

🌡 *Cool* ❂ *Bright* ❀ *Perfumed*

***Cymbidium* England's Rose 'Geyserland'** is a selection developed by Andy Easton, who has been responsible for some of the finest hybrid cymbidiums over the past two decades. The flowers of these modern hybrids will often last for two months in fine condition.

***Cymbidium* Fifi 'Harry'** *(left)* is a robust plant that produces long sprays of fragrant blooms, a legacy from its parent, the Australian species *C. madidum*.

🌡 *Intermediate* ❂ *Bright* ❀ *Perfumed*

🌡 *Cool* ☀ *Bright* ❀ *Perfumed*

***Cymbidium* Jubilation 'Geronimo'** is a highly awarded cultivar that has been given a First Class Certificate from the Australian Orchid Council.

🌡 *Cool* ☀ *Bright* ❀ *Perfumed*

***Cymbidium* Gigli 'Gold'** is an eye-catching intermediate style hybrid (it blooms halfway in size between the miniature and standard *Cymbidium* hybrids) that is a very vigorous grower. The color is unusual for this hybrid combination.

🌡 *Cool* ☀ *Bright* ❀ *Perfumed*

***Cymbidium* (Katydid × Supreme Destiny) 'Val Shipway'** is at present an unregistered intermediate hybrid, with clean, pale green flowers and a predominantly white labellum.

🌡 *Cool* ❁ *Bright* ❀ *Perfumed*

🌡 *Cool* ❁ *Bright* ❀ *Perfumed*

🌡 *Cool* ❁ *Bright* ❀ *Perfumed*

Cymbidium **Little Bighorn 'Ulladulla'** proves that deep green flowers can be striking, especially when they have contrasting colors in the lip.

Cymbidium **Paddy Mouse 'Geyserland'** is another example of the wide range of colors that are available in today's hybrid cymbidiums.

Cymbidium **Red Adair 'Launceston'** is a well-shaped dark bloom, which has an eye-catching white border to the flower, accentuating the maroon color.

🌡 *Cool* ❁ *Bright* ❀ *Perfumed*

🌡 *Cool* ❁ *Bright* ❀ *Perfumed*

Cymbidium **Mavourneen 'Jester'** is a novelty standard hybrid that is unusual in having the labellum colors also transposed onto the petals. These are referred to as peloric types.

Cymbidium **Royale Fare 'Krista'** is a standard cymbidium that has won many prizes. The flower color can vary between yellow and green—depending on how much light the developing buds receive.

Cool ❋ Bright ❁ Perfumed

***Cymbidium* Shifting Sands 'Gingerman'** is another example of some of the newer colors being developed in standard cymbidiums.

Cool ❋ Bright ❁ Perfumed

***Cymbidium* Tonto's Target 'Royale'** is one of the newer intermediate hybrids that display their blooms above the foliage.

Cool ❋ Bright ❁ Perfumed

***Cymbidium* Winter Fire 'Trudy Kay'** is an example of a red intermediate style hybrid.

Cool ❋ Bright ❁ Perfumed

***Cymbidium* Spotted Leopard 'Royale'** is an unusual standard hybrid that has fine spotting over the entire bloom.

Cool ❋ Bright ❁ Perfumed

***Cymbidium* Wallmurra 'Jupiter'** is a hybrid developed in Australia that has won many prizes because of its good shape and dark pink to red–purple color.

DENDROBIUM

(from the Latin dendron = tree, and bios = life, living on a tree) (pronounced: den-DRO-bee-um)

The genus *Dendrobium* has always been popular because of its diversity and generally free-blooming characteristics. The genus enjoys a wide distribution, from India and Sri Lanka, through Southeast Asia to New Guinea, Australia, and the Pacific Islands. They are almost exclusively epiphytes or lithophytes, with a sympodial growth habit. This genus is so large, with over 1,300 taxa and complex, that the species have been placed into smaller sub-groupings known as sections. There is an amazing diversity of plant habit, flower form, and color in this large genus. Almost all colors and combinations are represented in the flowers. It contains species, whose individual blooms last for only a few hours, to others that can persist for up to nine months in pristine condition. A number of species produce aerials or "keikis" from the older pseudobulbs. The majority of flowers marketed as "Singapore Orchids" are *Dendrobium* hybrids. These are generally warm-growing hybrids derived from the sections *Phalaenanthe*, *Spatulata,* and *Latouria*. *Dendrobium nobile* and related species have been used to create the thousands of colorful and long-lasting hybrids, which enjoy bright light and cool to warm conditions. These fragrant-flowered hybrids perform well on sunny window ledges in a bark-based medium.

🌡 *Intermediate* ✹ *Semi-shade*

Dendrobium ceraula is endemic to the Philippines, where it grows in mountainous forests. It prefers cool, moist, shady conditions, and produces flowers that vary in color from blue-mauve through pink to white, with a flat, purple striped labellum. This species was previously known as *D. gonzalesii.*

🌡 *Warm* ✹ *Bright*

🌡 *Cool* ✹ *Bright*

Dendrobium bigibbum is the popular "Cooktown Orchid" from north Queensland, Australia and New Guinea. It has spectacular, 1½-inch (40-mm) purple blooms, on sprays of up to 20 flowers. It has been the backbone of the *Phalaenanthe*-style *Dendrobium* breeding. It likes warm conditions, and must be kept dry when dormant in winter. *D. phalaenopsis* is a closely related species.

Dendrobium chrysanthum is a pendulous species that can grow over 40 inches (1 m) long. It flowers in the fall, along the nodes opposite the thin leaves, and blooms while in full leaf; then sheds the foliage immediately after flowering. It has round, orange enameled flowers, with two dark, blood red blotches on the lip, that last just over a week. It occurs from India to Indochina.

Intermediate ⚘ Semi-shade

Dendrobium chrysopterum is a recently described species from New Guinea that was previously misinterpreted as *D. obtusisepalum*. Its large and outstanding orange and yellow blooms are produced in spring, and these flowers last for almost two months.

Dendrobium engae is a robust species from the mountains of New Guinea, in Enga Province. It is a member of section *Latouria*, and has large flowers that can last for up to four months.

Intermediate ⚘ Semi-shade

Cool ⚘ Semi-shade

Cool ⚘ Semi-shade ✿ Perfumed

Dendrobium cuthbertsonii is one of the gems of the orchid world, with individual blooms that can last up to nine months under favorable conditions. It is a miniature plant from the highlands of New Guinea with disproportionately large blooms. It comes in a range of bright colors, including, red, orange, yellow, pink, white, plus bicolor forms utilizing these colors. It is a cool growing species, which prefers a narrow range in temperature, away from the extremes of winter and summer. In cultivation, they must be kept moist, and *Sphagnum* moss is frequently used for potted plants.

Dendrobium falcorostrum is a cool growing species, from mountainous regions of eastern Australia (near the New South Wales and Queensland border). In the spring, it has short sprays of perfumed white to cream flowers.

Intermediate ☼ *Bright* ❀ *Perfumed*

Dendrobium goldschmidtianum is a bright purple-flowered species, from Taiwan and northern parts of the Philippines. From late winter to summer, it has clusters of up to twenty blooms, about 1 inch (25 mm) in diameter, that grow from the leafless pseudobulbs. *D. miyakei* is a synonym.

Cool ☼ *Semi-shade* ❀ *Perfumed*

Dendrobium gracilicaule is a slender, spring flowering, fragrant species from eastern Australia. It has small arching spikes of yellow-green flowers, which are heavily blotched with red-brown on the back of the segments.

Cool ☼ *Bright* ❀ *Perfumed*

Dendrobium kingianum is a highly variable, popular, spring flowering, lithophytic species from eastern Australia. Up to twelve, 1-inch (25 mm), fragrant flowers are produced from the compact plants. Colors vary from pure white, through most shades of pink to deep beetroot purple. The labellum is white, blotched, and splashed with purple. Many superior cultivars have been developed, through selective line breeding of desirable forms. It is an ideal beginner's orchid, and has played an important role in hybridization.

Intermediate ✿ *Semi-shade*

Dendrobium lawesii is a member of the colorful *Calyptrochilus* section of *Dendrobium*. Most of these species have bright, tubular flowers with an upturned tip to the labellum, and a semi-pendent, leafy growth habit. *D. lawesii* certainly rivals *D. cuthbertsonii* for the range of colors exhibited in this species, which are mainly bird pollinated. *D. mohlianum*, from parts of the Pacific Islands, is a similar species with dark orange flowers.

Dendrobium macrophyllum *(below)* is a warm growing lowland species that is found in parts of Indonesia, New Guinea, and the Pacific Islands. It is another member of section *Latouria* that flowers for weeks or months. An interesting feature is that the seed capsules on this orchid are covered in long bristles.

Warm ✿ *Bright*

Intermediate ✿ *Semi-shade*

Dendrobium melinanthum is a scarce species from New Guinea, related to *D. lawesii*. Bright orange flowers, without any other colors, are rare in orchids. The flowers can last for over eight weeks on the plant, which can bloom at various times throughout the year.

Cool ✿ *Bright* ✿ *Perfumed*

Dendrobium nobile is a variable species throughout its range from India to southern China. It varies in color from deep purple to pure white, with many shades and bi-colored combinations in between. *D. nobile* is an excellent beginner's orchid as there are some lovely cultivars available, such as *D. nobile* var. *nobilius* (large deep purple), *D. nobile* var. *virginale* (pure white), and *D. nobile* var. *cooksonianum* (unusual, with the labellum coloring in the petals). All of these plants are in section *Dendrobium,* and have been used to create a number of "softcane" hybrids. Other species used have been *D. aureum* (plus the distinct *D. heterocarpum*), *D. friedericksianum* (yellow flowers), *D. signatum* (formerly known as *D. hildebrandii*), *D. regium* (soft pink flowers), the tri-colored *D. wardianum,* and the unusual *D. findlayanum* with knobbly pseudobulbs.

Dendrobium smillieae is a warm growing species, known as the "Bottlebrush Orchid," from lowland areas of northeastern Australia and New Guinea. It has densely packed clusters of blooms that vary in color from white to pinkish green, with a dark, bottle green labellum.

🌡 *Warm* ✷ *Bright*

🌡 *Intermediate* ✹ *Bright* ✿ *Perfumed*

Dendrobium speciosum is a highly variable orchid from eastern Australia, with many populations recognized as varieties, subspecies, or species in their own right. Including subsp. *speciosum*, subsp. *hillii*, subsp. *grandiflorum*, subsp. *capricornicum*, subsp. *curvicaule,* and subsp. *pedunculatum*. It is known as the "Rock Lily," or the more appropriate "King Orchid," and is a popular garden plant in frost-free climates. It blooms from late winter to spring, with large inflorescences of white to deep yellow, and highly fragrant flowers. It is a robust plant, with large specimens, and is an unforgettable sight when seen in full bloom.

🌡 *Intermediate* ✹ *Semi-shade*

Dendrobium tapiniense is a robust species from New Guinea that is from the section *Latouria*. The individual blooms are very thick and can last for up to three months.

***Dendrobium* Akatuki 'G2'** is an example of one of the hybrids that have large percentages of *D. nobile* in their ancestry.

Dendrobium tetragonum comes from eastern Australia in a range of forms, sizes, and colors. It has semi-pendulous pseudobulbs, which are distinctly four-angled in cross-section. It has spidery blooms, from 1 to 6 inches (25 to 150 mm) tall, which are cream to yellow green, often with dark purple to brown blotches and borders on the floral segments. The labellum can be white or marked with brown to purple spots or striations. It predominantly blooms in spring and summer.

Dendrobium victoriae-reginae is endemic to mountainous forests in the Philippines, and is one of the few "blue" orchids. Up to four, 1½-inch (40-mm) lilac to dark blue-purple flowers are produced, on short sprays, from nodes along the branching pseudobulbs. It prefers cool, moist conditions, and flowering occurs throughout the year.

🌡 *Warm* ✴ *Bright*

Dendrobium Aropa is a section *Latouria* hybrid between the related *D. johnsoniae* and *D. forbesii*, made by the late G. Hermon Slade.

🌡 *Intermediate* ✹ *Bright*

**Dendrobium Bohemian
Rhapsody** is a floriferous primary
hybrid developed from the compact
species *D. loddigesii* and the pendent
D. aphyllum (that was previously
well known as *D. pierardii*).

🌡 *Intermediate* ✹ *Bright*

Dendrobium Brinawa Sunset
is a cross between *D.* Peewee
(*tetragonum* × *bigibbum*) and
D. falcorostrum, referred to as
"hot/cold" hybrids because they
have both warm and cool growing
species in their background.

🌡 *Intermediate* ✹ *Bright*

Dendrobium Austasia is an
unusual hybrid between the Asian *D.
fimbriatum* (probably the var. *oculatum*)
and the Australian *D. tetragonum*.

🌡 *Intermediate* ✸ *Bright*

Dendrobium **Dawn Marie 'GJW'**
is an outstanding cultivar of
the primary hybrid between
D. formosum and *D. cruentum*, which
are both known as "nigrohirsute"
dendrobiums because of the fine
black hairs on the pseudobulbs.

🌡 *Cool* ✸ *Bright*

Dendrobium **Dorrigo 'Wisteria'**
is an unusual colored "softcane"
cultivar that was developed in
Australia.

Dendrobium **Elated 'Cairns'** is
an intersectional hybrid (hybrid
between distantly related species
from different sections) made
by Kevin McFarlane between
D. macrophyllum and *D.* Fiftieth
State (New Guinea [*macrophyllum*
× *atroviolaceum*] × *phalaenopsis*).

🌡 *Warm* ✸ *Bright*

Dendrobium Felicity Fortescue 'Pink Lady' is a very floriferous "softcane" cultivar with long lasting blooms.

🌡 *Cool* ☼ *Bright* ✿ *Perfumed*

🌡 *Intermediate* ☼ *Bright*

Dendrobium Formidable is another "nigrohirsute" primary hybrid, between the closely related *D. formosum* and *D. infundibulum*.

🌡 *Intermediate* ☼ *Bright*

Dendrobium Frosty Dawn is a compact growing, second-generation "nigrohirsute" hybrid that was developed by H & R Nurseries in Hawaii.

Dendrobium Gatton Sunray is a large growing hybrid that enjoys bright light. It is *D.* Illustre (*chrysotoxum* × *pulchellum*) backcrossed onto *D. pulchellum*.

🌡 *Intermediate* ✺ *Bright*

🌡 *Cool* ✺ *Bright* ✿ *Perfumed*

🌡 *Cool* ✺ *Bright* ✿ *Perfumed*

🌡 *Cool* ✺ *Bright* ✿ *Perfumed*

Dendrobium Graeme Banks 'Greta' is a hybrid between *D.* Sunglow (*speciosum* × *fleckeri*) and *D.* Hilda Poxon (*speciosum* × *tetragonum*), made by the author, David Banks and named after his father.

Dendrobium Hagaromo 'Spring Fuji' is a pastel pink and white "softcane" cultivar that blooms in late spring, after most similar hybrids have finished flowering.

Dendrobium Hambuhren Gold 'Magic' is a popular "softcane" cultivar because of its unusual color, which deepens as the flower ages.

🌡 *Warm* ☀ *Bright*

Dendrobium Hot Lips is an example of a typical section *Phalaenanthe* hybrid crossed with one of the "petaloid" hybrids similar to *D.* Kuranda Classic, expressing characteristics intermediate between the parents.

🌡 *Warm* ☀ *Bright*

Dendrobium Maid of Gloucester is an example of a "spatulata" or "ceratobium" *Dendrobium* hybrid that has highly twisted petals. It is a primary hybrid between *D. tangerinum* and *D. canaliculatum*.

Dendrobium Kuranda Classic is an example of a "petaloid" section *Phalaenanthe* hybrid that has the labellum taking on the character of another petal.

🌡 *Warm* ☀ *Bright*

🌡 *Cool* ☀ *Bright* ❀ *Perfumed*

Dendrobium My Noble Lady 'Purple Tips' is one of the older "softcane" cultivars that has the appearance of a much improved *D. nobile*.

🌡 *Cool* ✷ *Bright* ✤ *Perfumed*

Dendrobium **Orange Gem** is a strong colored "softcane" cultivar with a major influence of *D. aureum* in its background.

🌡 *Cool* ✷ *Bright* ✤ *Perfumed*

Dendrobium **Red Fairy 'Akebono'** is another brightly colored "softcane" cultivar that has different colors in the lip.

🌡 *Cool* ✷ *Bright* ✤ *Perfumed*

Dendrobium **Pink Doll 'Magic'** shows the impact a mature "softcane" hybrid can make when in full bloom, creating a "tower of flowers."

🌡 *Cool* ✷ *Bright* ✤ *Perfumed*

Dendrobium **Ruby Blossom 'Red King'** is one of the darkest "softcane" hybrids that have been produced.

🌡 *Cool* ✷ *Bright* ✤ *Perfumed*

Dendrobium **Sailor Boy 'Pinky'** is a popular and delightful soft pink "softcane" cultivar that has fragrant blooms.

Cool ❀ *Bright* ❀ *Perfumed*

Dendrobium Specio-kingianum 'Sid Burton' is a fine example of the hybrid between the Australian species, *D. speciosum* and *D. kingianum*, that was first made over a century ago. Natural hybrids also occur in the wild and are known as *D.* × *delicatum*.

Warm ❀ *Bright*

Dendrobium Thai Pinky is one of the hybrids used extensively for cut flower production, with a high percentage of *D. phalaenopsis* in its ancestry.

Dendrobium Stardust 'H & R' *(below)* is an unusual "softcane" hybrid that gets its style from the influence of the species *D. unicum*.

Intermediate ❀ *Bright*

🌡 *Warm* ✲ *Bright*

Dendrobium White Fairy is an important cut flower, which are often sold in florist shops as "Singapore orchids," and seen in restaurants and hotel foyers.

Dendrobium Wonga is an Australian *Dendrobium* hybrid between *D. speciosum* and *D.* Hastings (*kingianum* × *fleckeri*).

🌡 *Cool* ✲ *Bright* ❀ *Perfumed*

🌡 *Warm* ✲ *Bright*

Dendrobium Thanaid Stripes is a distinctive section *Phalaenanthe* style hybrid that has *D. bifalce* in its background, which is responsible for the striping.

 *Cool* ✹ *Bright* ✿ *Perfumed*

Cool ✹ *Bright* ✿ *Perfumed*

Dendrobium Yodogimi 'No. 1' is one of the many "softcane" cultivars developed by Jiro Yamamoto in Japan and Hawaii, who has been the leader in breeding these orchids over many decades.

Dendrobium Yondi Tina 'Goliath' is the only Australian *Dendrobium* hybrid to have received the highest honor of a First Class Certificate, as well as winning the Ira Butler Gold Trophy.

DOCKRILLIA

(after Alick Dockrill, an Australian author and orchidologist) (pronounced: DOCK-rill-ee-ah)

Dockrillia is an Australian and New Guinean genus of 30 species, with outlying populations throughout parts of the Pacific Islands. It is a recent genus and loosely accommodates the "terete-leaved" *Dendrobium* species. The main characteristics, which separate *Dockrillia* from *Dendrobium* include a lack of pseudobulbs, succulent leaves (which are often terete, or round in cross-section), and flowers appearing upside down, with the labellum uppermost. They are very easy plants to grow. The larger, pendent species grow well on generous slabs of treefern or cork, where they will be happy for many years. Some of the species, which clump at the base, may be grown in small pots or wooden baskets in a bark-based medium. They have a vigorous root system which prefers not to be disturbed. They grow and bloom in quite strong light and will take a wide range of temperatures.

🌡 *Cool* ☀ *Bright* ✿ *Perfumed*

🌡 *Cool* ☀ *Bright* ✿ *Perfumed*

🌡 *Intermediate* ☀ *Bright* ✿ *Perfumed*

Dockrillia linguiformis makes a great foliage plant, known as the "Tongue Orchid" or "Thumbnail Orchid." This species, from eastern Australia, now becomes the type for *Dockrillia*. It produces short sprays of feathery white blooms in spring.

Dockrillia teretifolia is arguably the most outstanding species in the genus. To see mature plants in full bloom is an unforgettable sight, giving rise to the common name of "Bridal Veil Orchid." It produces masses of white to greenish-cream, slender, feathery blooms in late winter to early spring. It is native to coastal regions of eastern Australia.

Dockrillia wassellii is an adaptable species from northeastern Australia. It prefers sunny window ledges but can withstand cool temperatures for short periods. It has attractive, succulent, erect leaves. These produce up to 50 densely flowered, slender, white blooms on upright inflorescences. The labellum is yellow and the plants bloom spasmodically during the warmer months.

EPIGENEIUM

(from the Greek epi = upon, and geneion = chin, referring to the raised calli on the labellum of some species) (pronounced: eh-pee-GEEN-ee-um)

This genus of sympodial orchids is found in mountainous regions of Southeast Asia. There are some very desirable horticultural subjects, and 35 or so species are in cultivation. They are related to *Dendrobium* and enjoy similar conditions. Many have a climbing growth habit and it's therefore more suitable to mount them on large rafts rather than plant them in pots. Shallow saucers or hanging baskets have also been successfully used for these plants.

Epigeneium treacherianum is the most impressive species of the genus. It has long spikes with up to 20 (rarely more), 2-inch (50-mm,) widely opening and starry blooms that are watermelon purple, with lighter tips to the segments. It is from the Philippines and Borneo. *Epigeneium lyonii* is a synonym.

🌡 *Intermediate* ✲ *Semi-shade*

EPIDENDRUM & RELATED GENERA

EPIDENDRUM

(from the Greek epi = upon, and dendron = tree, referring to the epiphytic habit of most species)
(pronounced: eh-pee-DEN-drum)

This is a large genus from Central and South America with over 500 members. Despite new species being discovered, this genus is declining as the various sections of taxa are taken out and given generic status. Gardeners will be familiar with the "Crucifix Orchids," which are actually reed-stem *Epidendrum* species and their hybrids. The various species come from a range of altitudes, and there are therefore representatives to suit most frost-free gardens. Some species have a dormancy period, but most are in continual growth. They generally require bright light and warm conditions, with some of the more vigorous "reed stem" types suitable for pot culture on patios in full sun. Some of the smaller growing species are well suited to bright, sunny window ledges.

🌡 *Intermediate* ✲ *Bright* 🏵 *Perfumed*

Epidendrum ciliare looks like a *Cattleya* in growth habit, but without the telltale floral sheath. It is a variable species from Central America, which can produce inflorescences of up to eight large, spidery green flowers, with a white labellum. It needs strong light, and a dry winter rest to bloom.

🌡 *Intermediate* ✲ *Shade*

Epidendrum barbeyanum is a compact growing plant with fleshy, green flowers that can often blend in with the color of the foliage. It is native of Central America.

🌡 *Intermediate* ✲ *Bright*

Epidendrum ibaguense is a common and widespread species from Mexico to Colombia. It is the classic reed-stem "Crucifix Orchid," which (including its hybrids) is popular in horticulture. It has globose heads of orange to red blooms with a modified yellowish labellum. Plants require strong light, and in favorable conditions will bloom throughout the year. There are a number of related species, including *E. cinnabarinum, E. imatophyllum,* and *E. radicans.*

 Warm ✺ *Shade*

Epidendrum ilense is an amazing species that is endemic to coastal Ecuador. It has bizarre flowers, with bland green petals and sepals, and a highly specialized white labellum that is fringed with long, fine hairs. This showy species demands constant warm, moist conditions. Large plants may constantly be in flower, as they rebloom from the same stem for many years.

🌡 *Cool* ✺ *Semi-shade*

Epidendrum parkinsonianum is a pendulous growing species from Mexico to Panama. It is worth growing just for its succulent, purple-stained foliage. Older plants can grow up to 7 feet (2 m) long. It produces up to three large, 4¾-inch (120-mm), greenish flowers with a pure white labellum. *Epidendrum falcatum* is a similar species, which differs by having a distinct pseudobulb behind the leaf, and slightly smaller blooms. Both of these species are best grown on large slabs, or allowed to hang from small wooden baskets.

🌡 *Intermediate* ✵ *Semi-shade*

Epidendrum pfavii is a tall reed-stem type from Costa Rica. It has long-lasting blooms that vary in color from magenta to brilliant cerise, which reproduce on the long inflorescences.

🌡 *Warm* ✵ *Semi-shade*

***Epidendrum* Costa Rica** is a tall-growing, colorful hybrid between *E. schumannianum* and *E. pseudowallisii*.

🌡 *Intermediate* ✵ *Bright*

***Epidendrum* Cosmo Dream Color** is one of the reed stem hybrids with the crucifix shaped labellum. These can be grown in the garden in most frost-free zones.

🌡 *Intermediate* ✵ *Bright*

***Epidendrum* Hokulea 'Santa Barbara'** is an improved cultivar that was bred in Hawaii. The flowers are much larger and last longer than some of the smaller species in its background.

🌡 *Warm* ✵ *Semi-shade*

***Epidendrum* Susquehanna** is a warm-growing hybrid between *E. pseudepidendrum* and *E. pseudowallisii*, which accounts for its unusual color combination. Mature plants can grow up to 40 inches (1 m) tall.

AENCYCLIA

(from the Latin enkyklein = to include, referring to the side lobes of the labellum that surround the column) (pronounced: en-SIK-lee-ah)

This is a complex genus of about 150 taxa from Central and South America, of generally intermediate to warm-growing species. They often grow in clumps and have a distinct pseudobulb. Recently, sections of *Encyclia* have been transferred to separate genera. For example in 1998, a large group of the "Cockleshell" encyclias was moved into the genus *Prosthechea*. They are easily recognized by their "upside down" flowers, and a labellum that displays varying degrees of dark purple striation. Many are also highly fragrant. *Encyclia* are readily grown, either on cork slabs or potted in a well-drained medium. Most species have a dormant period from late fall to early spring. The majority of the species are summer flowering.

Encyclia cochleata is an easily grown and variable species that is common in Central and South America. It has slightly twisted, green-yellow petals and sepals, and a very dark, purple-black labellum. The larger plants can bloom over a few months. *Encyclia cochleata* var. *alba (left)* is the rare albino form of the species, and was recently reclassified as *Prosthechea cochleata*. It is the national flower of Belize.

Intermediate *Bright* *Perfumed*

Intermediate *Bright* *Perfumed*

Encyclia osmantha is a Brazilian species that sometimes is confused with the related *E. megalantha*. The flowers are sweetly scented and last for over six weeks on the plant.

🌡 *Intermediate* ✹ *Bright* ❀ *Perfumed*

🌡 *Cool* ✹ *Bright* ❀ *Perfumed*

Encyclia prismatocarpa is found from Costa Rica to Brazil. It has upright inflorescences with blooms that are yellow-green and overlaid with deep maroon spotting. This species was recently reclassified as *Prosthechea prismatocarpa*.

Encyclia radiata is a popular, highly fragrant summer-flowering species, from Mexico, Guatemala, and Honduras. It has long-lasting, waxy, creamy green flowers, with a pale labellum, highlighted with some fine mauve veins. This species was recently reclassified as *Prosthechea radiata*.

EPIPHRONITIS

(a bi-generic hybrid between Epidendrum and Sophronitis) (pronounced: eh-pee-FRON-eye-tiss)

This is one of the first bi-generic hybrids, registered in 1890 between *Epidendrum* and *Sophronitis*. They prefer more shade and cooler conditions to most epidendrums, and a mixture that retains more moisture. They tend to be in constant growth throughout the year, and do not have a distinct rest period.

***Epiphronitis* Veitchii** is the primary hybrid between *Epidendrum radicans* and *Sophronitis coccinea*. It grows best in small pots and makes an attractive specimen in bloom.

🌡 *Cool* ✹ *Semi-shade*

LYCASTE & RELATED GENERA

LYCASTE

(from the Greek liquate = daughter of Primes, referring to the plant's beauty)
(pronounced: lie-CAST-ee)

These deciduous sympodial orchids are native to coastal and mountainous regions from Mexico to Peru, and there are about 50 species in total. They are cool to warm-growing epiphytes or terrestrials with fat pseudobulbs and large, thin, plicate leaves. Many of the Central American species (particularly the highly scented, yellow-flowered group), often leave sharp spines after the previous seasons' leaves have fallen. They are best grown in pots, as their roots must not dry out during the growing season. During this active growth, they are heavy feeders and require copious watering. The sepals open fully in most species, with the petals pushed forward and often adjacent to the labellum. The solitary flowers bloom in spring and summer, coinciding with the new growth of the plant. These grow on erect stalks from the base of the pseudobulb, and some species are known to produce these flowers in generous numbers. There are many hybrids within this genus, including *L. Koolena*, *L. Macama*, and *L. Shoalhaven*. These are mostly based on the cool growing species *L. Skinneri*, which is a highly desirable and variable epiphytic species from Guatemala (where the rare white-flowered form is the National flower), Honduras, and El Salvador. It has large, 4¾ inches (120 mm), light to deep pink blooms.

🌡 *Cool* ✳ *Shade*

Lycaste trifoliata is a lithophytic (and sometimes terrestrial) species from South America. It has green flowers and a white labellum that is heavily fringed along its margin.

🌡 *Cool* ✳ *Semi-shade* ✿ *Perfumed*

Lycaste deppei is an easily grown, spring-flowering species from Mexico to Nicaragua. It has 3½-inch (90-mm) pale green blooms, which are overlaid with heavy red-brown spotting. The petals are pure white, and the labellum is orange with red spots.

🌡 *Cool* ✳ *Shade*

Lycaste locusta has delightful, slightly nodding, dark bottle-green blooms on tall scapes. It is a native of mountainous forests in Peru, and must be grown in cool to intermediate conditions.

🌡 *Cool* ✳ *Semi-shade*

***Lycaste* Shoalhaven 'Virgin White'** is a fine example of an *L. skinneri* hybrid, and actually looks like an improved form of the species. Most of these have flowers that range from pale to deep pink, however the above cultivar is an albino form.

BIFRENARIA

(From the Latin bi = two, and fermium = bridle, referring to the four pollinate that are separated on two stems) (pronounced: bi-FREN-air-ee-ah)

This is primarily a Brazilian genus of about 20 species related to *Lycaste* and *Maxillaria*. Some taxonomists still include the quite distinct multifloral and smaller bloomed *Stenocoryne* within *Bifrenaria*. Most bifrenarias have robust pseudobulbs with a single leathery leaf. They are adaptable to a wide range of temperatures, and quickly grow into specimen plants if conditions are suitable. They will take bright light and may not bloom if grown in shaded conditions. Many have large showy flowers that are fragrant. They bloom in spring and summer.

‡ *Intermediate*   ✪ *Semi-shade*

Maxillaria fractiflexa is a large-flowered species with spidery blooms from Colombia. It has narrow petals and sepals, and varies in color from dull gold to brown. It is a cool-growing species, suited to pot culture.

Bifrenaria harrisoniae from Brazil is a variable, late spring-flowering species that is popular in cultivation. It has off-white to yellow-cream blooms, supplemented with a purple lip that is covered in fine silky hairs, which can be up to 3½ inches (90 mm) across. There is also an albino form (with pure white blooms and yellow at the base of the labellum) that is easier to flower.

‡ *Cool*   ✪ *Bright*   ✿ *Perfumed*

‡ *Cool*   ✪ *Shade*

Maxillaria sanderiana is a spectacular species from the moist, cool cloud forests of Ecuador and Peru. It is best grown in wire baskets, using *Sphagnum* moss as the medium. This allows the large, 4¾-inch (120-mm), pendent blooms, which are cream with deep red blotches at the base of the segments, to penetrate through the base of the basket in summer.

MAXILLARIA

(from the Latin maxilla = jaw-bone, referring to the labellum that in some species looks like a protruding chin) (pronounced: max-ill-AIR-ee-ah)

This is a complex group of over 700 distinct epiphytes and lithophytes from Central and South America, exhibiting an enormous range in plant habit and floral shape, size, and color. They have solitary blooms, that grow from the base of the pseudobulbs, and the petals are smaller than the sepals. Being such an assorted group of sympodial orchids, they have varying cultural requirements. However, most of the species established in cultivation are cool to intermediate-growing plants that enjoy bright light. They grow well in pots of a coarse, bark-based mix and the miniature species grow particularly well on slabs of treefern or cork. Some of the larger flowered species (*M. sanderiana, M. striata*) have blooms reminiscent of *Lycaste*, and need to be grown in baskets because of their often pendant flowering habit.

PESCATOREA

(after J.P. Pescatore, a French orchid enthusiast) (pronounced: pess-KAT-or-ee-ah)

This is a small genus with about 15 species of epiphytic orchids, which occur from Costa Rica to Colombia. They have fan-shaped growths, and require humid, shaded, intermediate conditions throughout the year without a rest period. Pescatoreas need to be kept moist, as they have no pseudobulbs for water storage. Constant fresh, moving air around the thin foliage is a necessity. The large, colorful, fragrant, and long-lived blooms are most attractive and appear singly from the leaf axils, in spring and summer.

🌡 *Intermediate* ✲ *Shade*

Pescatorea cerina is from Panama and Costa Rica. It has highly fragrant, creamy white to pale lemon yellow blooms, with broad segments. The labellum is yellow with some fine, dark red, longitudinal stripes.

🌡 *Intermediate* ✲ *Shade*

Pescatorea lehmannii is from Colombia and Ecuador. It has white flowers that are longitudinally striped with maroon on the petals and sepals. The labellum is dark purple, covered in cream bristle-like hairs.

PROMENAEA

(after the Greek princess, Promeneia) (pronounced: prom-en-EYE-ah)

This is a genus of about 12 impressive miniature species, from central and southern Brazil, with proportionally large flowers that are produced singly at the base of the plant. They are sympodial plants with clustered pseudobulbs, related to *Zygopetalum*. They enjoy cool to intermediate temperatures, under moist and shaded conditions. Mature plants will have numerous blooms in season, overhanging the edge of the pot. *Sphagnum* moss or fine-grade bark is a suitable medium, and they must not be over potted. They bloom in spring and summer. *Promenaea stapelioides* has 2-inch (50-mm) blooms, which are greenish yellow and densely blotched and barred with purple red. The circular and flat labellum is solid black-purple in color. *Promenaea xanthina* has bright yellow, 2-inch (50-mm) flowers, with fine red spotting on the labellum. It blooms in summer. *P. citrina* is a synonym.

🌡 *Cool* ✲ *Shade*

Promenaea Goldspeck is a hybrid that gets the yellow tones from the *P. xanthina* parent, while the spotting comes from *P. stapelioides* that is in the background of *P.* Norman Gaunt.

ZYGOPETALUM

(from the Latin, zygos = yoke, petalum = petals, referring to the petals and sepals which are fused to the column foot) (pronounced: zy-go-PET-a-lum)

This is a small genus of about 20 species of terrestrials and epiphytes from South America. They have tall spikes of large, showy, long-lasting and highly fragrant flowers. Zygopetalums are hardy orchids that enjoy similar conditions to cymbidiums, and are often grown together. They like to be grown in deep pots, to accommodate the vigorous root system. The plants respond to frequent watering and feeding throughout the year. There have been many hybrids made, within both *Zygopetalum* and related genera, to produce compact plants that expand and intensify the color range of the blooms.

🌡 *Cool* ✹ *Bright* ✿ *Perfumed*

Zygopetalum intermedium is a Brazilian species. It has fleshy, green petals and sepals that are blotched with maroon purple. The fan-shaped labellum is white, with dark lilac veining. Up to ten, 3-inch (75-mm), blooms are produced on thick, erect spikes in the fall and winter. *Z. mackayi* is a related species.

Zygopetalum **Titanic** *(left)* is a robust hybrid that is highly fragrant. Such plants can quickly fill a room with their pleasant bouquet.

🌡 *Cool* ✹ *Bright* ✿ *Perfumed*

WOODWARDARA

(after Beverley Woodward, Australian orchid grower) (pronounced: wood-ward-AR-ah)

This is a recently registered genus, which is a tri-generic hybrid between *Colax* (now correctly known as *Pabstia*), *Neogardneria*, and *Zygopetalum*. Culture is similar to that recommended for zygopetalums, except that the plants require more shade and moisture.

🌡 *Cool* ✹ *Semi-shade* ✿ *Perfumed*

Woodwardara **Beverley Lou** produces green flowers with petals and sepals that are striped with deep maroon markings, and a white labellum suffused with lilac.

ZYGOCASTE

(a bi-generic hybrid between Zygopetalum and Lycaste) (pronounced: zy-go-CAST)

This is an unusual hybrid combination between *Zygopetalum* and *Lycaste*. These types of hybrids rarely produce fertile seed, so such successful combinations should be multiplied by using the latest tissue culture techniques. They require the same cultural conditions as their parents.

Zygocaste **Northwest Passage 'Touch of Irish'** is a rare hybrid between *Zygopetalum* Artur Elle and *Lycaste skinneri*. It has upright sprays of up to five flowers with a shape between the parents.

🌡 *Cool* ✹ *Semi-shade* ✿ *Perfumed*

ZYGOCOLAX

(a bi-generic hybrid between Zygopetalum and Colax) (pronounced: zy-go-KOW-lax)

This is a hybrid combination between *Zygopetalum* and *Colax* (now correctly known as *Pabstia*). These are more compact plants than many of the zygopetalums, and have the advantage of blooming more than once a year.

Zygocolax **Gumeracha** is a fourth generation hybrid with the species *Zygopetalum maxillare, Zygopetalum intermedium, Zygopetalum crinitum,* and *Pabstia jugosa* (as *Colax jugosus*) in its background.

❄ *Cool* ✲ *Semi-shade* ✿ *Perfumed*

ZYGONERIA

(a bi-generic hybrid between Zygopetalum and Neogardneria) (pronounced: zy-go-NEAR-ee-ah)

This is a hybrid combination between *Zygopetalum* and *Neogardneria*. The green color of the hybrid progeny invariably comes from the species *Neogardneria murrayana*. Culture is similar to that recommended for zygopetalums, except the plants require more shade and moisture.

❄ *Cool* ✲ *Semi-shade* ✿ *Perfumed*

Zygoneria **Adelaide Meadows 'Emma'** has five species in its background, which are *Zygopetalum crinitum, Z. maxillare, Z. intermedium, Z. mackayi,* and *Neogardneria murrayana*. It can bloom twice a year.

❄ *Cool* ✲ *Semi-shade* ✿ *Perfumed*

Zygoneria **Dynamo** is one of the parents of *Zygoneria* Adelaide Meadows, with its shape heavily influenced by *Neogardneria murrayana*.

MASDEVALLIA & RELATED GENERA

MASDEVALLIA

(after Dr. Jose Masdevall, a Spanish botanist) (pronounced: mas-de-VAL-ee-ah)

This is a large genus of around 500 tufted epiphytes and lithophytes from Central and South America. They are generally plants of the cloud forests, in mountainous regions, that thrive throughout the year. Masdevallias have no pseudobulbs, and store moisture in their roots and fleshy leaves. There are species that bloom throughout the year, with the peak seasons being winter and spring. Most are single-flowered, with the smaller taxa making up for their small stature by the number of blooms they produce. In most cases, the larger-flowered species produce fewer blooms. They come in an amazing range of shapes, sizes, and bright colors. The sepals often terminate with a short or long tail, while the petals and labellum are generally tiny. *Sphagnum* moss is the preferred medium for the culture of these sympodial orchids, which must be kept moist, shaded, and cool throughout the year.

Masdevallia ionocharis is a cool-growing species from Peru. It is a scarce species in the wild, but now plants are being raised from seed to supply the demand for this colorful epiphyte.

🌡 *Cool* ✺ *Semi-shade*

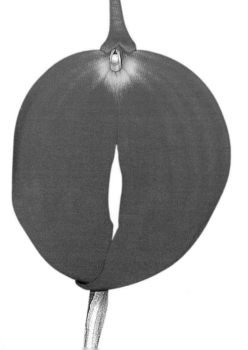

Masdevallia coccinea is a spectacular species from Colombia. In the summer it grows large, round flowers on tall scapes, above the foliage. It is most variable in color, ranging from all shades of red, purple, pink, yellow, and white.

🌡 *Cool* ✺ *Semi-shade*

🌡 *Cool* ✿ *Semi-shade*

Masdevallia *tovarensis* is a delightful white-flowered species from Venezuela. It has small bunches of up to four long-lived flowers, and can rebloom from the same inflorescence the following season. It is more warmth-tolerant than many of the other species.

🌡 *Cool* ✿ *Semi-shade*

Masdevallia *veitchiana* is a majestic large-flowered species from Peru, and is well known to visitors to the ancient Aztec city of Machu Picchu. It has tall spikes, longer than the leaves, of orange flowers, which are covered with minute bright purple tubercles, giving the bloom an incandescent sheen in sunlight. This species is frequently used in hybrids.

🌡 *Cool* ✿ *Semi-shade*

Masdevallia Angelita 'Royale' is a very floriferous hybrid with three different species in its background, being *M. sanctae-inesae, M. strobelii,* and *M. veitchiana.*

🌡 *Cool* ✿ *Semi-shade*

Masdevallia Angle Dangle is the result of the cross between *M.* Harlequin and *M. angulata,* an unusual combination that has fleshy and slightly nodding blooms.

🌡 *Cool* ☸ *Semi-shade*

***Masdevallia* Baby Doll** is one of
the newer hybrids that show how
floriferous these plants can be in
very small pots, often blooming
only a year or two out of flask.

🌡 *Cool* ☸ *Semi-shade*

***Masdevallia* Falcata** is an old
primary hybrid between *M. coccinea*
and *M. veitchiana* that has been
remade many times by a number of
hybridists. It is one of the most
popular and boldly colored hybrids.

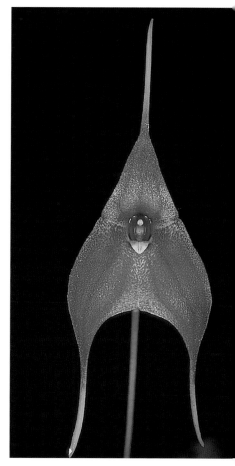

🌡 *Cool* ☸ *Semi-shade*

***Masdevallia* Velveteen Angel** is a
primary hybrid between *M. uniflora*
and *M. panguiensis* that has neon
purple blooms on wiry stems.

🌡 *Cool* ☸ *Semi-shade*

***Masdevallia* (Copper Angel ×
Minaret)** is an unregistered hybrid
that has the distinct striping that is
so popular with orchid enthusiasts.

🌡 *Cool* ☸ *Semi-shade*

***Masdevallia* Harlequin** is a
very pretty and distinctive hybrid
between two very cool-growing
orchids—*M. calocodon* and
M. uniflora. These plants resent
high temperatures and will readily
shed their leaves if the growing
conditions are not to their liking.

DRACULA

(from the Latin, dracula = little dragon, referring to the face in the center of the bloom)
(pronounced: drak-you-LA)

These are cool-growing orchids, that were previously included within the genus *Masdevallia*. The majority occur in the moist cloud forests of western Colombia and Ecuador. Due to this proximity to the Equator, there are no 'seasons,' so the plants experience the same weather conditions and day-length all year. In cultivation, they demand cool conditions and will quickly deteriorate if the conditions do not suit. Draculas do not like daytime temperatures rising above 79°F (26°C), and prefer a nighttime minimum of 54°F (12°C). They also require constant air movement and high humidity. Most successful growers cultivate their plants in live *Sphagnum* moss. Because many species have a descending inflorescence, suspended baskets or mesh pots are best. Shade seems to suit most species—especially if they are being cultivated in a warm climate. The blooms collapse in high temperatures, but can be rehydrated by misting with cold water.

🌡 *Intermediate* ✿ *Shade*

Dracula robledorum has flowers covered in small hairs. It has a yellow to cream bloom, heavily overlaid with fine dark purple to chocolate blotches that converge into stripes. Like most Draculas, it is sequentially flowered. It is native to Colombia.

🌡 *Intermediate* ✿ *Shade*

Dracula vampira is the most famous species, because of its name alone! This Ecuadorian species has exceedingly dark, purple-brown striped flowers, which from a distance appear black. It can have blooms up to 8½ inches (215 mm) tall, although they are often smaller. There have been increasing numbers of *Dracula* hybrids being produced, which are easy to grow.

🌡 *Intermediate* ✿ *Shade*

Dracula dalstroemii is an attractive, large, 9½-inch (240-mm), flower species from Ecuador. It has creamy blooms, suffused with light brown markings.

🌡 *Intermediate* ✿ *Shade*

Dracula gorgona is an attractive, large 7-inch (175 mm) and hairy flowered species from Colombia. It has white and yellow blooms, overlaid with a dense network of red-purple, oval spots. It is closely related to *D. chimaera*.

DRACUVALLIA
(a bi-generic hybrid between Dracula and Masdevallia) (pronounced: drak-you-VAL-ee-ah)

This is a manmade combination between the genera *Masdevallia* and *Dracula*. Cultivation is the same as that recommended for masdevallias.

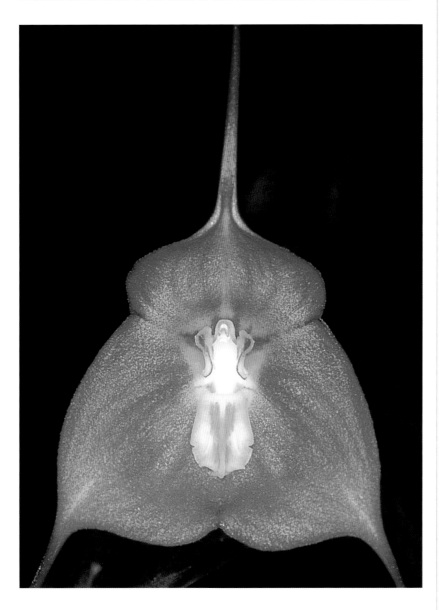

***Dracuvallia* Blue Boy 'Cow Hollow'** *(left)* is a primary hybrid between *Masdevallia uniflora* and *Dracula chimaera* that has richly colored flowers that appear to glow.

🌡 *Cool* ✹ *Shade*

Lepanthes stenophylla is from Guatemala, where it grows at an altitude of around 4,600 feet (1,400 m) above sea level. It needs to be kept constantly moist, and healthy plants will bloom throughout the year.

🌡 *Cool* ✹ *Shade*

LEPANTHES
(from the Latin, lepis = scale, anthos = flower, referring to the tiny flowers) (pronounced: le-PAN-theez)

This is a large group of some 1,000 distinct, diminutive epiphytes from Central and South America, which are related to *Pleurothallis*. These small-growing botanicals are commonly native to high-altitude mist forests, and demand cool, humid, and heavily shaded conditions. They are generally grown in small pots of *Sphagnum* moss or mounted on cork or treefern slabs, and require frequent watering.

PLEUROTHALLIS

(from the Latin, pleuros = rib, thallos = shoot, referring to the flattened stems, or ramicauls found in this genus) (pronounced: plu-ro-THA-liss)

This is a very large genus of over 1,200 sympodial orchids from the American tropics. They are generally epiphytes of the mountainous rainforests, however there are many species that grow in open situations, on rocks, or as terrestrials, generally in thick mosses. A single-leaf is produced, frequently on a thin, flattened "stem," correctly called a ramicaul, as they lack pseudobulbs. The flowers are produced from a spathe or sheath at the base of the leaf, either singly or on an inflorescence. Some of the smaller-flowered examples have individual blooms that could be mistaken for members of the unrelated genus, *Bulbophyllum*. Plants range from miniatures to species that can grow over 40 inches (1 m) tall. Most are cool-growing, however there are examples from lowland regions that require warm conditions in cultivation. They generally tolerate a wide range of temperatures and strong light intensity. Most species may be grown in *Sphagnum* moss, with some of the creeping species suitable for mounting on treefern.

Pleurothallis viduata is a mysterious species from Ecuador. It has only been collected in the wild once, and unfortunately has never been relocated. It is a vigorous and easily grown plant that blooms throughout the year, especially in the warmer months. It produces single pure white flowers, with two deep maroon spots on hair-like spikes.

Cool ✸ *Shade*

ONCIDIUM & RELATED GENERA

ONCIDIUM

(from the Latin onkos = mass, swelling, referring to the warty callus at the base of the labellum)
(pronounced: on-SID-ee-um)

This genus of over 400 species from tropical America, includes numerous sections with their own generic rank. *Cyrtochilum* and *Psychopsis* are examples, as well as the flattened-leafed group of oncidiums transferred into the genus *Tolumnia*. Oncidiums produce yellow and brown flowers on long, branching inflorescences and are most eye-catching when in full bloom. In many species, the labellum is the most prominent feature. The species is frequently grown mounted, which permits unimpeded development of the root system, and allows for quick drying after watering. Some of the smaller species may be grown in pots. The cultural requirements are varied, and depend largely on the habitat and altitude of the particular species. The majority of species prefer intermediate to warm-growing conditions.

🌡 *Warm* ☀ *Bright*

Oncidium sphacelatum is a vigorous species from Central America that is adaptable in cultivation, enjoying a wide range of temperatures and humidity levels. It has long, branched, and upright to arching inflorescences, of typical brown and yellow blooms. It is a very hardy and reliable species that can be grown outside in frost-free climates.

Oncidium gardneri is a summer-flowering Brazilian species, with a branching inflorescence of pale brown and yellow blooms. *O. crispum, O. enderianum,* and *O. forbesii* are related brown-flowered species.

🌡 *Cool* ☀ *Bright*

Oncidium varicosum is the "Dancing Lady Orchid," from Brazil and neighboring countries. It is a fall-flowering species, with upright, branching inflorescences of up to seventy 2-inch (50-mm) blooms, which are long lasting. It has small petals and sepals that are yellow with brown markings, but the labellum is the outstanding feature. The lip is large, flat, round, bright yellow, and simply dominates the flower. This species has been dominant in the production of "*varicosum*-type" *Oncidium* hybrids.

🌡 *Cool* ✺ *Shade*

🌡 *Intermediate* ✺ *Bright*

Oncidium Killer Bees is a recent hybrid that has three different species in its makeup: O. *concolor,* O. *marshallianum,* and the uncommon O. *viperinum.*

Oncidium Margaret Reid 'Lemon' is a rare example of an albino form of a "*varicosum*-type" hybrid. Many thousands of seedlings need to be flowered for a chance of this unusual color.

🌡 *Cool* ✺ *Bright*

🌡 *Warm* ✺ *Bright*

🌡 *Cool* ✺ *Bright*

***Oncidium* Palmyre 'Lynette'** is a typical example of a "*varicosum*-type" hybrid, as *Oncidium varicosum* accounts for almost 80 percent of its background. It enjoys bright light in cool to intermediate conditions, and blooms in the fall.

🌡 *Intermediate* ✺ *Bright* ✾ *Perfumed*

***Oncidium* Memoria Bill Carter** is a hybrid with only two species in its parentage, *Oncidium papilio* and *O. sanderae*. Its major influence, *O. papilio,* is the "Butterfly Orchid" from the West Indies and tropical parts of South America. It has large flowers, up to 6 inches (150 mm) tall, that are produced singly on a tall, flattened inflorescence. It will flower off the same spike for many months. They have a very narrow,

and predominantly brown dorsal sepal and petals, and broader lateral sepals that are yellow and brown banded. The labellum is wide, flat, and brown, centered with a large pale yellow blotch. *Psychopsis,* now the correct genus name for this type of *Oncidium,* also has attractive foliage.

***Oncidium* Sweet Sugar** is another hybrid with *O. varicosum* influence, however it is more tolerant of higher temperatures due to infusions of *O. flexuosum* and *O. sphacelatum.* While it will grow well in a pot of course bark, growing it on slabs of cork or tree fern requires less maintenance.

***Oncidium* Twinkle 'Fragrance Fantasy'** is a dainty and floriferous hybrid between the small yellow *O. cheirophorum* and the pink *O. ornithorhynchum* from Central America. It has branched and pendant spikes of pale flowers, which smell of chocolate. The individual blooms are 1 inch (25 mm) tall, and long lasting. This hybrid will withstand a wide temperature range and grows well in *Sphagnum* moss.

🌡 *Intermediate* ✽ *Semi-shade* ✿ *Perfumed*

BRASSIA

(after William Brass, an English botanist) (pronounced: BRASS-ee-ah*)*

This genus of some 25 species from tropical America is popular in cultivation. The large, and often perfumed, spidery blooms, are presented on arching inflorescences which can grow to over 11 inches (280 mm) from tip to tip. Many of the species are from the lowlands and like warm, moist, and bright conditions. They grow well in pots with a bark-based medium. The vigorous hybrid *Brassia* Rex (*verrucosa* × *gireoudiana*) is worth cultivating, although it generally grows into a large plant before it actually flowers. *Brassia* has also been used in hybrids with related genera such as *Miltonia, Odontoglossum,* and *Oncidium.* Some species, traditionally placed within *Brassia,* have since been included within the genus *Ada.*

Brassia verrucosa is from Mexico and Venezuela and performs well in shadehouse conditions in frost-free zones. It is a reliable late spring bloomer, producing its large, spidery, pale green fragrant flowers, with fine dark green spotting at the base. The smaller-flowered *B. brachiata* is often included within this species.

🌡 *Cool* ✽ *Bright* ✿ *Perfumed*

MILTONIOPSIS

(From Miltonia and Greek opsis = resemblance, referring to the similarity to the genus Miltonia)
(pronounced: mil-ton-ee-OP-sis)

This small genus of only five or six species is primarily from Colombia and Ecuador, and was once included within *Miltonia*. There have been many hybrids created within this showy genus, known as the "Pansy Orchids." The two main species in the background of today's hybrids are *Miltoniopsis phalaenopsis* and *M. vexillaria*. These orchids prefer a narrow temperature range. They do not tolerate below 50°F (10°C) in winter, or above 78°F (26°C) in summer. The thin, glaucous foliage burns readily in strong light, so they prefer a shaded position. The flat blooms bruise easily, and will readily mark if not provided with ample air movement. They should be grown in small pots, with *Sphagnum* moss used exclusively as the growing medium.

Miltoniopsis **Dick Richenbach 'Fiona'** has up to several fragrant flowers growing from each inflorescence. Each seedling has a slightly different "mask" in the center of the bloom.

🌡 *Intermediate* ✹ *Shade* ✿ *Perfumed*

***Miltoniopsis* Evergreen Pride 'Devonport'** *(above)* is an example of the impressive floral display these "pansy orchids" provide.

***Miltoniopsis* Grouville 'Ben'** shows how hybridists have aimed for an oval-shaped bloom.

***Miltoniopsis* Hamburg 'Bambi'** is one of the older hybrids that has been widely cultivated due to its strong growth, outstanding color, and free-flowering habit.

***Miltoniopsis* Jean Carlson** is a classic hybrid with hot pink blooms. These are ideal flowering pot plants, which last in bloom for many weeks.

ODONTOGLOSSUM

(from the Latin odontos = tooth and glossa = tongue, referring to the two tooth-like humps on the base of the labellum) (pronounced: oh-dont-oh-GLOSS-um)

Odontoglossums are cool-growing orchids from mountainous regions of South America, related to *Oncidium* and *Miltoniopsis*. They have short to long spikes of large, showy blooms. Most of the 60 species have yellow and brown flowers that are often spidery. The most popular ornamental subjects are those species with white and pink flowers, and wider segments which give the effect of a round bloom. They do not like their roots to dry out, so the plants need to be potted. They are suitable for cool-growing conditions, and require abundant water throughout the year. There are numerous hybrids within *Odontoglossum* and with related genera. Some of the most popular include *Colmanara* (× *Miltonia* × *Oncidium*), *Odontioda* (× *Cochlioda*), and *Odontocidium* (× *Oncidium*). They all enjoy similar growing conditions.

🌡 *Cool* ✹ *Semi-shade*

Odontoglossum Roy Hipkins 'Royale' is a hybrid made by Robert Hamilton of California, USA. The solid brightness of color is outstanding in this award winning cultivar. It has large percentages of *O. crispum* and the yellow and brown *O. triumphans* in its background.

🌡 *Cool* ✹ *Semi-shade*

Odontoglossum crispum is the undisputed queen of the genus, and is endemic to Colombia. It can have over 12 large, widely opening blooms with broad segments, and often rounded and finely serrated edges. The color varies from sparkling white to pale rose, variously spotted or blotched with red or purple.

 *Cool* ✸ *Semi-shade*

Odontoglossum Mimosa *(left)* is one of the older hybrids with a labellum heavily influenced by *O. harryanum.*

🌡 *Intermediate* ✸ *Semi-shade*

Odontoglossum wyattianum *(right)* is a distinctive species from Peru and Ecuador, growing in mossy cloud forests at around 6,650 feet (2,000 m). It is closely related to *O. harryanum.*

ROSSIOGLOSSUM

(after J. Ross, who collected orchids in Mexico) (pronounced: ross-ee-oh-GLOSS-um)

This small group of Central American species was at one time included under *Odontoglossum.* Only six different species are recognized. Due to their color and floral features, they have become known as "Tiger" or "Clown Orchids." They appreciate warm, moist conditions and bright light during their main growing period, from late spring to fall. Flower spikes develop from late summer to fall and blooming takes place during late fall and winter. During the winter months, they need to be kept on the dry side, and only watered enough to keep the pseudobulbs from shriveling. They are best grown potted, in a bark-based mix, and under intermediate conditions.

Rossioglossum grande is from Mexico and Guatemala. It has stiff spikes of up to eight flowers, between 5½ inches (140 mm) across, which are yellow with chestnut-brown bars across the sepals, and yellow and brown petals. The labellum is creamy with dark red-brown markings. Its main flowering season is in winter.

🌡 *Intermediate* ✸ *Bright*

COLMANARA

(after Sir Jeremiah Colman, early English orchid hybridizer) (pronounced: kol-MAN-ar-rah)

This is a tri-generic hybrid combining *Miltonia, Odontoglossum,* and *Oncidium.* Cultivation is as for odontoglossums, however these hybrids are more warmth tolerant, and are successful in cool, intermediate, and warm conditions.

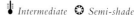

Intermediate ❁ *Semi-shade*

***Colmanara* Wildcat 'Carmela'** is arguably the most successful *Colmanara* hybrid to date, due to the vigor of the plants and the wide range of colors throughout the original seedlings.

***Colmanara* Wildcat 'Gemma Webb'** is a stunning example of one of the deepest blood red varieties.

Intermediate ❁ *Semi-shade*

ODONTOCIDIUM

(a bi-generic hybrid between Odontoglossum and Oncidium) (pronounced: oh-dont-oh-SID-ee-um)

This combination of *Odontoglossum* and *Oncidium* makes these plants suitable for growing indoors and outside in warmer zones. They often have tall spikes of medium sized flowers which grow in impressive numbers.

🌡 *Intermediate* ✲ *Semi-shade*

***Odontocidium* Dorothy Wisnom 'Golden Gate'** is one of the finest odontocidiums, developed by Tom Perlite of California, USA. It has large infusions of *Odontoglossum crispum, Oncidium leucochilum,* and *Oncidium tigrinum* in its ancestry.

ODONTIODA

(a bi-generic hybrid between Odontoglossum and Cochlioda) (pronounced: oh-dont-ODE-ee-ah)

This is a cool growing bi-generic hybrid between *Odontoglossum* and *Cochlioda.* The South American *Cochlioda noezliana* has imparted its bright red color to many of its hybrids.

Odontiodas do not like their roots to dry out, so the plants need to be potted. They are suitable for cool growing conditions, and require abundant water throughout the year and a semi-shaded position.

🌡 *Intermediate* ✲ *Semi-shade*

***Odontioda* Aissa McLaughlin** *(left)* shows the intensity of color inherited from *Cochlioda noezliana.*

***Odontioda* Margarete Holm** has its unusual color derived from the Central American species, *Odontoglossum rossii* and *O. bictoniense.*

🌡 *Cool* ✲ *Semi-shade*

Cool ❁ *Semi-shade*

Odontioda Omeo 'Sophie' is one of the outstanding hybrids developed by Director of the Australian Orchid Foundation Gerald McCraith.

Odontioda Pescoleyn 'Keith Ryan' has a distinctive mottled pattern to the flower, which makes every bloom unique.

Cool ❁ *Semi-shade*

VUYLSTEKEARA

(after Mr C. Vuylsteke, a Belgian orchid grower) (pronounced: vul-STEEK-ee-ar-rah)

This is a tri-generic hybrid involving *Cochlioda*, *Miltonia*, and *Odontoglossum*. The crossing of *Odontioda* with *Miltonia* has formed these colorful hybrids.

Vuylstekearas do not like their roots to dry out, so the plants need to be potted in *Sphagnum* moss or a fine bark mix. They are suitable for cool-growing conditions, and require abundant water throughout the year and a semi-shaded position.

Vuylstekeara Memoria Hanna Lassfolk highlights the variation within this genus once three different genera become involved.

Cool ❁ *Shade*

Cool ❁ *Shade*

Vuylstekeara Edna 'Stamperland' is an older hybrid that has medium-sized vibrantly colored flowers on tall inflorescences.

WILSONARA

(after a Mr Wilson, an early English hybridist) *(pronounced: wil-SON-ar-rah)*

This is a tri-generic hybrid involving *Cochlioda*, *Odontoglossum*, and *Oncidium*. Generally the crossing of *Odontioda* with *Oncidium* has formed these colorful hybrids, which are more tolerant of higher temperatures than most of the pure odontoglossums.

Wilsonara **Firecracker 'Red Star'** *(below)* as blooms that last for up to two months.

🌡 *Cool* ❂ *Semi-shade*

🌡 *Cool* ❂ *Semi-shade*

Wilsonara **Russiker Tiger 'Lisette'** is a hybrid heavily influenced by *Oncidium tigrinum*.

PAPHIOPEDILUM & RELATED GENERA

(from the Greek pedilon = slipper, referring to the pouch-like modified labellum) (pronounced: paff-EE-oh-ped-ee-lum)

The Asiatic "Slipper Orchids" have long been highly prized in horticulture, with their distinctive modified pouch-like labellum. They are cultivated throughout the world, and countless hybrids have been produced from the 90 or so different species. The range of *Paphiopedilum* extends from India, eastward across southern China to the Philippines, and throughout Southeast Asia and Malaysia, to New Guinea and the Solomon Islands. New species continue to be discovered, particularly in remote rainforest areas of Indonesia, China, and Vietnam. There is huge diversity within the genus. Some species are terrestrial, growing through the leaf litter on the forest floor. While others are lithophytes, and show a preference for limestone cliffs. There are also a number of epiphytes, happy to live in the major forks of rainforest trees. Most produce a single flower, while some may have up to 12 or more open at one time, and others flower sequentially. They are found in sunny situations and the flowers, which come in a wide range of colors and form, often last well over a month in perfect conditions. Most of the species have plain green strap leaves, yet there are others with attractive mottled foliage. They do not have pseudobulbs but store water in their fleshy leaves and thick, hairy root system.

The Asiatic slipper orchids are best grown in pots, with a well drained, bark-based medium being most suitable. Select a pot size that fits the roots snugly, as they will not tolerate stagnant conditions around the root system. Pot the plant so that it is only slightly buried, a ½ inch (12 mm) is enough, as often the roots will push the plant out of the mix, and any exposed new roots can become dry and not develop further. They need to be kept moist during warmer months, and enjoy frequent misting of the foliage. Many of the multifloral species require a drier rest in winter, in combination with a significant drop in temperature. There are cool, intermediate, and warm-growing species.

There are three basic styles of hybrids popular with orchid enthusiasts. Firstly, the "Maudiae"-type hybrids (*Paphiopedilum* Maudiae is an antique primary hybrid, between *P. callosum* and *P. lawrenceanum*) have tessellated or patterned two-tone foliage and single blooms that have prominent stripes on the broad, white dorsal sepal. The "albino" types have green stripes on the dorsal, with green petals and pouch; the "coloratum" types are similar, with purple stripes; the "vinicolors" have deep beet-colored flowers and almost black stripes. Secondly, multifloral hybrids have increased in popularity, and feature larger-flowered, spectacular species, such as *P. rothschildianum, P. philippinense, P. stonei,* and, since its rediscovery, *P. sanderianum.* The third group is the "complex hybrids." Despite being developed for over a century, there is only a handful of species in their pedigree. They are mostly multiple generation hybrids, the results of ongoing selective breeding over many decades with high ratios of *P. insigne, P. spicerianum,* and *P. villosum,* with minor influences of *P. bellatulum, P. charlesworthii, P. druryi, P. exul,* and *P. niveum.*

🌡 *Intermediate* ✹ *Semi-shade*

Paphiopedilum bellatulum is from the northern border of Thailand and Myanmar (Burma). It has large white flowers with sizeable deep maroon spots. The very short flower stem lets the single bloom rest on the tessellated leaves.

🌡 *Intermediate* ✹ *Shade* 🌸 *Perfumed*

Paphiopedilum delenatii is a soft pink colored species, with a darker pouch. It was recently rediscovered in its native Vietnam. It has delightful, tessellated foliage.

🌡 *Intermediate* ✲ *Shade*

Paphiopedilum druryi is an isolated species, only known to exist in southern India. This distinctive, rare, semi-terrestrial has small sulfur-yellow blooms with a single, dark brown stripe down the center of the petals and dorsal sepal.

🌡 *Intermediate* ✲ *Semi-shade*

Paphiopedilum haynaldianum is a multiflowered species, endemic to the Philippines. The flowers are green, white, and mauve with dark red blotches. *P. lowii* is a related species from Peninsula Malaysia, Borneo, and Indonesia.

🌡 *Intermediate* ✲ *Shade*

Paphiopedilum henryanum is found in northern Vietnam and southern China, and was only uncovered in the late 1980s. This colorful species was discovered by, and named after, a convicted orchid smuggler!

Cool ❂ *Semi-shade*

Paphiopedilum insigne is a
commonly grown, variable, winter-
flowering species from Nepal and
northern India. It has glossy,
brownish yellow flowers with
spotting on the dorsal sepal.

Warm ❂ *Semi-shade*

Paphiopedilum rothschildianum is
endemic to Mount Kinabalu in
Sabah, Borneo. Up to five, dark
striped flowers are produced on an
upright spike. Each flower is up to
12 inches (300 mm) across the
extended petals. It is the most
impressive and majestic species in
the genus.

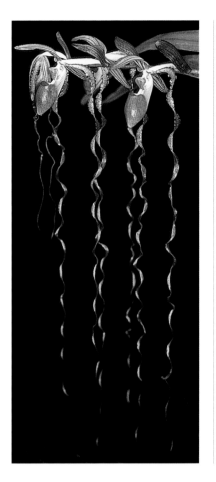

Warm ❂ *Semi-shade*

Paphiopedilum sanderianum is
endemic to Sarawak, Borneo. Up
to five, bizarre flowers are produced
on the inflorescence; which can
have individual blooms up to 37
inches (95 cm) tall! It is the largest
flowered species in the genus, and
their were even doubts about
its authenticity, until it was
rediscovered in the early 1980s.

Paphiopedilum spicerianum is from
northern India. It has olive green
undulating petals, a bronze pouch,
and a broad dorsal sepal, that is
white with a green base and a
narrow central purple stripe.

Cool ❂ *Semi-shade*

🌡 *Cool* ✹ *Semi-shade*

Paphiopedilum **Baulkham Hills 'Lynette'** is an example of one of the newer hybrids. The blooms on this flower last for over three months.

🌡 *Cool* ✹ *Semi-shade*

Paphiopedilum villosum is a common species from India to Indochina. It has very glossy flowers that have a bronze overlay. The dorsal sepal is green with dark brown markings at its base. The petals are actually two-tone; the top half is red-brown, with the bottom half yellow-green. *P. boxallii* is a closely related species, with darker, spotted flowers.

🌡 *Cool* ✹ *Semi-shade*

Paphiopedilum **Amanda 'Joyance'** is an older hybrid still used in hybridizing for its outstanding shape.

🌡 *Cool* ✹ *Semi-shade*

Paphiopedilum **Danella 'Chilton'** is a complex hybrid that has stood the test of time, being a consistent prizewinner since the late 1960s. The coloration and markings can be attributed to the influence of *P. villosum* in its background.

🌡 *Warm* ✲ *Semi-shade*

Paphiopedilum Dollgoldi 'Golden Horizon' is a primary hybrid between the yellow-flowered species *P. armeniacum* and the multifloral *P. rothschildianum*.

Paphiopedilum Fanaticum 'Gosford' is a shapely, colorful, and fragrant hybrid between two of the Chinese species, *P. micranthum* and *P. malipoense*.

🌡 *Intermediate* ✲ *Semi-shade* ✿ *Perfumed*

🌡 *Intermediate* ✲ *Semi-shade* ✿ *Perfumed*

Paphiopedilum Fumi's Delight 'Angels Cloud' is the primary hybrid between the yellow-flowered species *P. armeniacum* and the pink bubblegum orchid, *P. micranthum*. Both of these species are from China.

🌡 *Intermediate* ✲ *Semi-shade*

Paphiopedilum Gold Dollar is the primary hybrid between the yellow-flowered species *P. armeniacum* and *P. primulinum*.

🌡 *Intermediate* ✳ *Semi-shade*

Paphiopedilum Hells Chamber
is an unusual hybrid between the
species *P. chamberlainianum* (now
correctly *P. victoria-regina*) and the
complex hybrid *P.* Hellas.

🌡 *Warm* ✳ *Semi-shade*

**Paphiopedilum Henrietta
Fujiwara** is the primary hybrid
between the albino form of
P. haynaldianum and *P. primulinum*.
Up to six blooms are produced
sequentially over a period of
months.

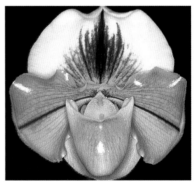

🌡 *Cool* ✳ *Semi-shade*

**Paphiopedilum Kathryn Cutler
'Lynette'** shows why these plants
are becoming increasingly popular
as houseplants, with their long-
lasting waxy flowers. This hybrid
was developed by Graeme Banks
OAM of Australia.

 Intermediate ✸ *Semi-shade*

Paphiopedilum Orchilla 'Chilton' is one of the classic complex hybrids. Registered in 1962, this clone is a major show winner because of its outstanding color and shape.

Paphiopedilum Oriental Venus 'Trim' is a "Maudiae-type" hybrid that also has the influence of *P. venustum*.

Intermediate ✸ *Semi-shade*

 *Warm* ✸ *Semi-shade*

Paphiopedilum Prince Edward of York 'WOC' is a multifloral primary hybrid between the classic species, *P. sanderianum* and *P. rothschildianum*. This plant was Reserve Champion at the 16th World Orchid Conference in Vancouver, Canada in 1999.

🌡 *Warm* ✳ *Semi-shade*

***Paphiopedilum* Shadowfax 'Vancouver Snow'** is one of the finest examples of modern white *Paphiopedilum* breeding, made by Terry Root of the Orchid Zone, California, USA.

🌡 *Warm* ✳ *Semi-shade*

***Paphiopedilum* Susan Booth 'Jannine'** is a fine example of the multifloral primary hybrid between *P. rothschildianum* and *P. praestans*. These hybrids tend to be summer flowering and last in bloom for up to two months.

🌡 *Intermediate* ✳ *Shade*

***Paphiopedilum* Silver Fleuret 'Geyserland'** is a fine example of the albinistic "Maudiae-type" hybrids. The tessellated foliage is an added bonus, and this style of hybrid grows well in the home. They need to be kept warm and moist with indirect filtered light.

🌡 *Warm* ✪ *Semi-shade*

***Paphiopedilum* Yellow Tiger 'Joan'** is a multifloral primary hybrid between *P. stonei* and *P. praestans*, which can grow into a sizeable plant.

***Paphiopedilum* Yospur** *(below)* is a hybrid between *P. conco-bellatulum* and *P. delenatii*, which retains the compact habit of its parents.

🌡 *Intermediate* ✪ *Semi-shade*

THE ORCHID DIRECTORY 181

PHRAGMIPEDIUM

(from the Latin phragma = partition and Greek pedilon = slipper, referring to the separate slipper-shaped labellum) (pronounced: frag-me-PEE-dee-um)

This genus of slipper orchids is from Central and South America, comprising some 20 species. The plants have plain green leaves and are multiple, generally sequential, flowering, with some robust species having branched spikes. Phragmipediums are well known from when their popularity skyrocketed in the early 1980s with the discovery of *P. besseae*. They have similar cultural requirements to those recommended for the related *Paphiopedilum*, however they like stronger light levels and appreciate frequent watering. Much success has been achieved by sitting the plants, which prefer deep, plastic pots, in shallow saucers of water, to a depth of up to 2 inches (50 mm). Two styles are very popular: the long-sepaled types, from *P. caudatum*, and the pink and red types, from *P. schlimii* and *P. besseae* respectively.

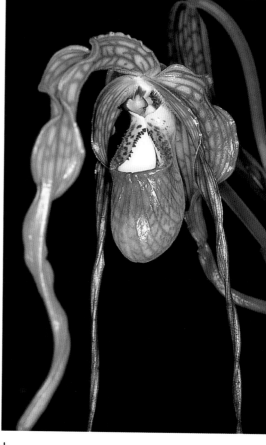

❄ *Warm* ☀ *Semi-shade*

Phragmipedium caudatum is the largest flowered member of the genus, and is found throughout Central and western South America. It has up to four, yellow-green to brown blooms, with long pendulous sepals that can be up to 23 inches (585 mm) long and ½ inch (12 mm) wide.

❄ *Intermediate* ☀ *Shade* ❀ *Perfumed*

Phragmipedium besseae is a spectacular species from Colombia, Ecuador, and Peru. It has orange to fire engine red flowers, with broad segments. There is also a rare, yellow form known as *Phragmipedium besseae* var. *flavum (right).*

❄ *Intermediate* ☀ *Shade* ❀ *Perfumed*

🌡 *Intermediate* ✲ *Semi-shade*

🌡 *Warm* ✲ *Semi-shade*

Phragmipedium xerophyticum *(left)* is a delightful but rare miniature species that sends out stolons that develop into new growths. It has tiny white flowers, and was only discovered in Mexico in the early 1990s. Some taxonomists reclassiy this under *Mexipedium xerophyticum.*

***Phragmipedium* Don Wimber 'Dennis Olivas'** is one of the finest of the present *P. besseae* hybrids. This is *P.* Eric Young crossed back onto the red *P. besseae.*

***Phragmipedium* Elizabeth March 'Suzanne'** is a compact-growing plant, well suited to indoor culture. They should have bright light and be kept moist.

🌡 *Intermediate* ✲ *Semi-shade*

🌡 *Intermediate* ✿ *Semi-shade*

🌡 *Intermediate* ✿ *Semi-shade*

***Phragmipedium* Eric Young 'Dale Hallberg'** is the primary hybrid between *P. besseae* and *P. longifolium.* Mature plants will bloom sequentially for many months.

***Phragmipedium* Hanne Popow 'Strawberry'** *(below)* is a strong colored cultivar from the primary hybrid of *P. bessae* and *P. schlimii.*

🌡 *Intermediate* ✿ *Semi-shade*

***Phragmipedium* Hanne Popow 'White Bubbles'** is another example of this hybrid showing the variation that can occur.

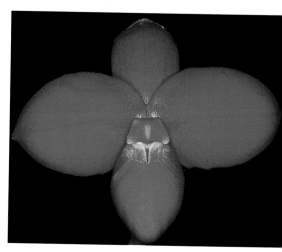

🌡 *Intermediate* ✿ *Semi-shade*

***Phragmipedium* Jason Fischer 'Bonne Nuit'** has a very strong *P. besseae* influence. It is *P.* Memoria Dick Clements (*sargentianum* × *besseae*) crossed back onto *P. besseae.*

Intermediate ✽ *Semi-shade*

***Phragmipedium* Noirmont 'Lava Flow'** is a vigorous growing hybrid with larger flowers. It is *P.* Memoria Dick Clements crossed with *P. longifolium.* Strong plants will often have a branched inflorescence.

***Phragmipedium* Saint Ouen 'Red Shift'** is *P.* Hanne Popow crossed back onto *P. besseae.*

Intermediate ✽ *Semi-shade*

PHALAENOPIS & RELATED GENERA

PHALAENOPSIS

(from the Latin phalaina = moth, opsis = looking like, referring to moth-like appearance of the flower) (pronounced: fal-eh-NOP-sis)

Phalaenopsis, known as "Moth Orchids," are found throughout the tropical rainforests of Southeast Asia. The 50 or so species occur as epiphytes, and the monopodial plants have only a few leathery leaves, which are often deep green. There are some species with attractive tessellated foliage. They require warm, humid, and damp conditions, with quite deep shade. These orchids are mostly grown in pots, however a number of the species perform well on long slabs. Many hybrids have been produced, and *Phalaenopsis* are of major commercial importance and among the most popular flowers, often used in wedding bouquets.

🌡 *Warm* ✲ *Shade*

Phalaenopsis equestris is a popular miniature-flowered species from the Philippines and Taiwan. It produces branched sprays of numerous pink to rose purple flowers.

🌡 *Warm* ✲ *Shade*

Phalaenopsis Algol 'Toska' is one of the novelty hybrids with a heavy influence from *P. amboinensis*.

🌡 *Warm* ✲ *Shade*

Phalaenopsis bellina is a native to Borneo and has green, white, and purple flowers that are produced from large plants that have glossy wide leaves. It was previously confused with the Malaysian *P. violacea*.

🌡 *Warm* ✳ *Shade*

Phalaenopsis City Girl is a delightful bi-colored hybrid, with white petals and sepals combined with a contrasting deep purple labellum.

🌡 *Warm* ✳ *Shade*

🌡 *Warm* ✳ *Shade*

Phalaenopsis Brother Showpiece *(above)* is an impressive striped, pink modern hybrid. These orchids are very popular as house plants.

Phalaenopsis Hwafeng Redqueen is a well-shaped dark pink to purple hybrid that blooms for up to eight weeks.

🌡 *Warm* ✳ *Shade*

🌡 *Warm* ✳ *Shade*

Phalaenopsis Carmela's Pixie 'Media Puzzle' is a smaller growing hybrid; with the influences of *P. equestris* and the pink spotted *P. stuartiana* coming through.

🌡 *Warm* ✳ *Shade*

Phalaenopsis Candy Kiss 'Jannine' is an outstanding example of a "candy-stripe" *Phalaenopsis*, with superb color definition.

Phalaenopsis Hybridizer's Dream 'Carmela' has won many awards because of its shape, arrangement and outstandingly rich color, with white border.

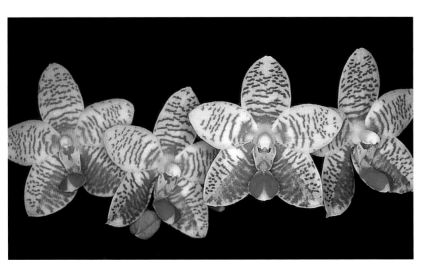

 Warm ✿ *Shade*

Phalaenopsis Orchid World
(above) is a highly awarded grex that
can bloom numerous times
throughout the year.

Phalaenopsis Pumpkin Patch
(above) proves that not all
Phalaenopsis are pink or white, with
this hybrid in the sunset tones.

 Warm ✿ *Shade*

 Warm ✿ *Shade*

**Phalaenopsis Spanish Dancer
'Harlequin'** is a bizarre cultivar
with a unique color combination
that defies explanation.

🌡 *Warm* ✲ *Shade*

***Phalaenopsis* Taisuco Flash** is another example of a "candy-stripe,' *Phalaenopsis* hybrid.

🌡 *Warm* ✲ *Shade*

***Phalaenopsis* White Lightning** is an example of the traditional white moth orchid, so popular with florists for weddings and other special occasions.

🌡 *Warm* ✲ *Shade*

***Phalaenopsis* Texas Mist 'Stephanie'** *(above)* is a hybrid heavily influenced by *P. amboinensis* and *P. violacea* (or possibly more correctly *P. bellina*).

***Phalaenopsis* World Class 'Big Foot'** has a semi-peloric labellum that gives the flower its distinctive look.

🌡 *Warm* ✲ *Shade*

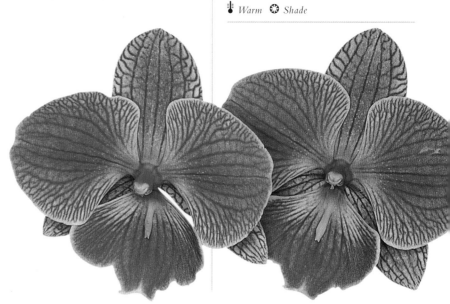

DORITIS

(from the Greek dory = spear, referring to the spear-shaped labellum) (pronounced: door-EYE-tis)

This is a genus of one, possibly two, semi-terrestrial, monopodial species from Southeast Asia, related to *Phalaenopsis*. They have an upright growth habit, with broad, succulent leaves, in two ranks that readily clump. They perform best potted in a well-drained medium, enjoy warm, humid conditions and will tolerate quite bright light.

Doritis pulcherrima has upright inflorescences that carry up to twenty 1-inch (25-mm) blooms, which vary in color from light pink to dark purple. It blooms in summer. There are also rare white, lilac (often termed "blue") and unusual splash-petalled cultivars.

🌡 *Warm* ✳ *Bright*

VANDA & RELATED GENERA

VANDA

(from the Indian language, Vanda is the term for this type of orchid) (pronounced: VAN-dah)

Vanda is a group of about 50 species of sturdy, monopodial orchids with representatives from Sri Lanka and India, across Southeast Asia to New Guinea and northeastern Australia. They are erect-growing, with strap-like, channeled leaves, in two ranks. Larger plants may branch at the base, and have numerous, very thick, cord-like roots. The inflorescences appear from the stem at the base of the leaf. They have showy, long-lasting blooms, which come in a range of colors and combinations. What were previously known as the "terete-leafed Vandas," have since been transferred to the genus *Papilionanthe*. This includes the popular *Vanda* Miss Joaquim, the national flower of Singapore. Vandas thrive in wooden baskets, in bright, humid, and intermediate to warm conditions.

🌡 *Warm* ✲ *Bright*

🌡 *Cool* ✲ *Bright*

🌡 *Cool* ✲ *Semi-shade*

Vanda coerulea is one of the best-known species, from the higher mountains of India through to northern Thailand. It has large, flat, and spectacular pale to deep lilac-blue, tessellated flowers, on erect spikes, frequently with over 12 blooms. It is a cool to intermediate-growing species, that is selectively line bred to accentuate the blue color and round shape.

Vanda javierae *(above)* is a rare and spectacular, recently discovered species from the Philippines. It has up to eight, 2½-inch (60-mm), white flowers with wide segments. It also has a white labellum that is anchor-shaped, with faint pink and brown markings at its base. It appreciates cool temperatures and filtered light.

Vanda sanderiana is one of the most magnificent orchid species from the Philippines. Some authorities consider that *Euanthe sanderiana* is the correct name for this species. It is a warm growing epiphyte that has been used extensively, like *V. coerulea*, in hybrids. A round-flowered species, it has up to ten, 4-inch (100-mm), blooms that are pink, with dark red-brown suffusions and tessellations on the lateral sepals. There is also an albino form, known as *Vanda sanderiana* var. *albata (top)*, with green and white flowers.

Intermediate ✵ *Bright*

Vanda tricolor is a distinctive common species, found on rocks or trees on the fringes of lowland forest in Java, Indonesia. It has perfumed white flowers, with dark red-brown spots. The labellum is purple, with yellow and white patches at its base.

Warm ✵ *Bright*

Vanda Marlie Dolera is a cross between one of the terete-leaved vandas and *V. sanderiana*. Such hybrids demand strong light to bloom well.

Warm ✵ *Bright*

Vanda Reverend Masao Yamada is a well-shaped, colorful hybrid whose characteristics have come from *V. sanderiana*.

Intermediate ✵ *Bright*

Vanda Sansai Blue is a deep blue hybrid with a heavy influence of *V. coerulea*.

AERIDES

(from the Latin, aer = air, referring to its epiphytic habit) (pronounced: air-EYE-deez)

The appropriately named *Aerides* (meaning "air-plant") are monopodial epiphytes that cling to their host by a few thick roots, with the remainder aerial. Many are sturdy plants found in the warm lowlands of Southeast Asia, however there are also species from the mountains. Most of the 20 or so species are easy to grow and have highly perfumed long-living flowers. *Aerides* enjoy high light levels and are mostly spring and summer blooming. They grow and display well in baskets. *Aerides* species can be cultivated in gardens in warm zones, attached to the trunks of suitable trees that do not shed their bark. In optimum conditions, the thick white roots will attach firmly to the host and ramble quite a distance from the plant. There have been many hybrids made between *Aerides* and other members of what are loosely termed the "vandaceous" family. Many of these hybrids come in a wide range of colors due to the high degree of genetic diversity.

Aerides odorata is widely distributed throughout Southeast Asia and is variable in color, from deep pink to pure white. Albinistic or white-flowered forms of these species are highly prized by collectors. It is an adaptable species, thriving out of doors in most frost-free zones. *A. lawrenciae* is a similar species (which is like a giant *A. odorata*), from the Philippines. It has longer leaves and much larger blooms.

🌡 *Intermediate* ☀ *Bright* ❀ *Perfumed*

ARACHNIS

(from the Latin, arachne = spider, referring to the spider-like thin segmented flowers) (pronounced: ah-RACK-nis)

Arachnis is a genus of about six species of scrambling monopodial epiphytes found throughout tropical lowland parts of Southeast Asia across to New Guinea. They demand full sun and hot, humid conditions to grow successfully, but they are difficult to confine to pots, and are best grown on trees in tropical gardens. The flowers are spider-like and long-lasting, and many of the popular intergeneric hybrids involve *Aranda* (× *Vanda*), *Aranthera* (× *Renanthera*), and the tri-generic *Mokara* (× *Ascocentrum* × *Vanda*).

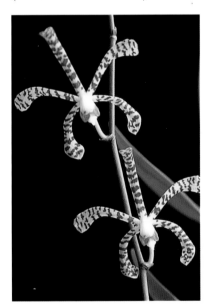

🌡 *Warm* ☀ *Bright*

Arachnis flos-aeris becomes a large scrambling plant with tall stems. It is found in Malaysia, Indonesia, and the Philippines. It demands full sun and hot, humid conditions for it to successfully bloom. They make ideal cut flowers and are long-lasting.

ASCOCENTRUM

(from the Latin, askos = bag and kentron = spur, referring to the large spur of the labellum)
(pronounced: as-koe-SEN-trum)

The monopodial genus *Ascocentrum* is a group of about eight small, compact plants that enjoy warm conditions and high light levels. They are ideal plants for wooden baskets and their colorful showy blooms are long lived. These Southeast Asian epiphytes have played an important part in the development of vandaceous hybrids. *Ascocentrum* has been bred with members of the genus *Vanda* to create the genus *Ascocenda*. The *Ascocentrum* has helped introduce bright colors to its progeny, while also reducing the plant size. They are mostly spring and summer flowering, but in the tropics, large plants can bloom throughout the year. These compact-growing and attractive plants are well suited to sunny window ledges, but keep an eye out for the roots, which will wander and attach themselves to timber or the walls.

❦ *Intermediate* ✿ *Bright*

Ascocentrum garayi with its bright orange flowers is a popular plant in its native Thailand, it also occurs in Indochina. Nurseries have selected horticulturally superior forms and have propagated these in large numbers from seed. This species has been confused with *A. miniatum*.

NEOFINETIA

(from the Greek, neo = new, and after Achilles Finest, a French botanist)
(pronounced: nee-oh-fe-NET-ee-ah)

This small-growing, monopodial genus from Japan and Korea is a distant relative of *Angraecum*. *Neofinetia* has one, possibly two species. They enjoy cool to intermediate-growing conditions, in bright light. Larger specimens grow well on cork slabs, and in terracotta pots, in gravel and bark mix. It has been the parent of some delightful, compact-growing and perfumed hybrids such as *Neostylis* Lou Sneary, the primary hybrid between *Neofinetia falcata* and *Rhynchostylis coelestis*.

❦ *Intermediate* ✿ *Semi-shade* ❀ *Perfumed*

Neofinetia falcata is considered a sacred plant in Japan. This is a variable species, with small clusters of up to ten fragrant white flowers with long spurs, which are produced on compact, clumping plants. The variegated leafed forms are highly prized.

RENANTHERA

(from the Latin, renes = kidney and anthera = anther, referring to the kidney-shaped pollinia)
(pronounced: ren-ANTH-er-rah)

Renanthera is a robust monopodial genus of some 15 species found throughout Malaysia, Indonesia, the Philippines, and New Guinea. Most species produce very bright long-lasting flowers on branched inflorescences. These tall-growing vandaceous epiphytes require warm to hot conditions with bright light. The Philippine species *Renanthera monachica* is a smaller plant that can cope with lower temperatures. There have been a number of hybrids made with related genera, particularly to exploit the bright red colors and improve the overall shape of the bloom.

Renanthera Monaseng has bright orange blooms that are heavily overlaid with red. It has *R. imschootiana, R. monachica,* and *R. storiei* in its pedigree.

🌡 *Warm* ☀ *Bright*

🌡 *Warm* ☀ *Bright*

Renanthera Tan Keong Choon is a striking red hybrid bred from the species *R. matutina, R. philippinensis,* and *R. storiei.*

SARCOCHILUS

(from the Greek, sarx = flesh, and cheilos = lip, referring to the fleshy labellum of the flower)
(pronounced: sar-koe-KY-lus)

This is a small genus of about 20 diminutive, monopodial epiphytes and lithophytes from eastern Australia, with outliers in New Caledonia. They are mostly spring and summer flowering, and have short inflorescences of showy blooms, which come in a wide range of shapes and colors. The main species in cultivation are the rock dwellers. In cultivation, these should be grown on long, narrow slabs. As a rule, they are clump-forming. The more popular combinations link the hardy lithophytic types (such as *S. ceciliae, S. fitzgeraldii,* and *S. hartmannii*) with the smaller-flowered, but colorful, epiphytic species. These hybrids are very easy to cultivate in pots, in a coarse mixture. A suitable mix is two parts medium-grade pine bark, one part of pea size gravel, and a handful of perlite. They appreciate shade and can take cool to cold conditions—almost down to freezing, but need protection from frost. Keep *Sarcochilus* moist, with good air circulation. There have also been a number of manmade, intergeneric hybrids involving *Sarcochilus*; some of the more popular are *Plectochilus* (× *Plectorrhiza*), *Rhinochilus* (× *Rhinerrhiza*), *Sarconopsis* (× *Phalaenopsis*), and *Sartylis* (× *Rhynchostylis*).

🌡 *Cool* ☀ *Bright*

Sarcochilus ceciliae is a lithophytic, pink-flowered species from northeastern Australia. It has up to 20, small, cup-shaped blooms, produced sequentially in summer. *S. eriochilus* and *S. roseus* are closely related species.

 *Cool* ✺ *Shade* ❀ *Perfumed*

Sarcochilus falcatus *(above)* is the most common species, being found as an epiphyte in rainforests along eastern Australia. It has up to 12, white to cream flowers, with varying degrees of gold and purple markings on the labellum.

Sarcochilus fitzgeraldii is a lithophytic species from mountainous parts of eastern Australia. It has up to a dozen, large white blooms with light pink to dark crimson spotting or banding in the center of the flower. It grows in cool and heavily shaded situations, and flowers in spring.

 Cool ✺ *Shade*

Cool ✺ *Semi-shade*

Sarcochilus hartmannii is a majestic lithophytic species, with its center of distribution being the coastal mountains of the New South Wales and Queensland border. It is a variable and highly sought-after orchid, with very thick leaves, which often grows in quite strong light. It has upright to arching sprays of up to 25, pure white, round flowers, with a tiny labellum, which may have varying degrees of reddish brown markings in the center of the bloom. The forms from 'Blue Knob' are almost pure white, whereas those from the nearby Numinbah Valley tend to have concentric circles and patterns of brownish red in the center. It flowers in mid to late spring.

ASCOCENDA

(a bi-generic hybrid between Ascocentrum and Vanda) (pronounced: as-koe-SEND-ah)

Ascocenda is one of the most popular genera in vandaceous orchids. They are hybrids between *Ascocentrum* and *Vanda*. The *Ascocentrum* has reduced the plant size significantly, injected a range of vibrant colors, and giving the blooms a rounder shape. They are erect, with strap-like, channeled leaves, in two ranks. Larger plants may branch at the base, and have numerous, very thick, cord-like roots. The inflorescences appear from the stem at the base of the leaf. They have showy, long-lasting blooms, which come in a range of colors and combinations. Ascocendas thrive in wooden baskets, in bright, humid, and intermediate to warm conditions. They also like sunny window ledges, as long as the plants are not subjected to cold temperatures in winter.

🌡 *Cool* ✺ *Shade*

Sarcochilus Weinhart is a small growing primary hybrid between *S. hartmannii* and the rare spotted epiphyte, *S. weinthalii*.

🌡 *Warm* ✺ *Bright*

Ascocenda Arcadia gets its size and shape from *Vanda sanderiana*, whereas the color is derived from *Ascocentrum curvifolium*.

🌡 *Warm* ✺ *Bright*

Ascocenda Carolaine 'Kathleen' is a different style of *Ascocenda*, with only one infusion of *Ascocentrum curvifolium* and five different *Vanda* species in its makeup.

PORTERARA
(after Abe Porter, an Australian orchid enthusiast) (pronounced: port-er-RAH-ra)

Porterara is a tri-generic hybrid involving *Rhynchostylis*, *Sarcochilus,* and *Vanda*. This new genus was created by Walter Upton, the Patron of the Australasian Native Orchid Society, to create "tropical"-style flowers on plants grown alongside his cool-growing *Sarcochilus*. He succeeded with this new combination that will grow in a wide range of conditions, from temperate to tropical. It therefore suits both cool and warm climates, as long as it is indoors and out of direct sunlight.

🌡 *Intermediate* ☼ *Semi-shade*

***Porterara* Blue Boy 'Jill'** is an outstanding awarded cultivar from the crossing of *Sartylis* Blue Knob (*Sarcochilus hartmannii* × *Rhynchostylis retusa*) and *Vanda coerulea*. It has the capacity to bloom a number of times throughout the year.

🌡 *Warm* ☼ *Bright*

***Ascocenda* Pramote** has bright orange blooms that last equally well on the plant or as a cut flower. Mature plants will bloom a number of times during the warmer months.

SARTYLIS

(a bi-generic hybrid between Sarcochilus and Rhynchostylis) (pronounced: sar-TIE-lis)

This hybrid was created to make many of the tropical vandaceous orchids more amenable to lower winter temperatures. At present there have only been about six of these hybrids registered, between *Sarcochilus* and *Rhynchostylis*.

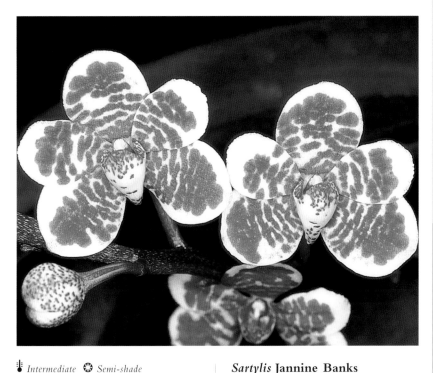

🌡 *Intermediate* ✿ *Semi-shade*

Sartylis **Jannine Banks 'Tinonee'** is an awarded example of the primary hybrid between *Sarcochilus hartmannii* and *Rhynchostylis gigantea*. It blooms repeatedly throughout the warmer months of the year.

VASCOSTYLIS

(a tri-generic hybrid between Ascocentrum, Rhynchostylis, and Vanda) (pronounced: vas-koe-STY-lis)

Most of the *Vascostylis* hybrids that have been registered are combinations of *Ascocenda* (*Ascocentrum* × *Vanda*) and *Rhynchostylis*. *Vascostylis* are erect, with strap-like, channeled leaves, in two ranks. Larger plants may branch at the base, and have numerous, very thick, cord-like roots. The inflorescences appear from the stem at the base of the leaf. They have showy, long-lasting blooms, which come in a range of colors and combinations. *Vascostylis* thrive in wooden baskets, in bright, humid, and intermediate to warm conditions and on sunny window ledges as long as the plants are not subjected to cold temperatures in winter.

🌡 *Warm* ✿ *Bright* ❀ *Perfumed*

Vascostylis **Precious 'Mikes Indigo'** is an award-winning cultivar owned by Robert Fuchs of R.F. Orchids in Florida, USA, one of the world leaders in Vandaceous breeding. This deeply colored clone is a hybrid between *Rhynchostylis coelestis* and *Ascocenda* Yip Sum Wah.

MISCELLANEOUS EPIPHYTIC GENERA

ACACALLIS

(from the Greek, Akakallis, the lover of Apollo. Many plant genera have been named after women in mythology) (pronounced: ak-ah-KAL-is)

Acacallis is a genus of only one species from Brazil, Venezuela, and Colombia. Its ascending habit means the plants are best grown on mounts of tree fern, as they will quickly wander out of the confines of a pot. They have thin leaves and prefer shady situations, with high humidity and intermediate to warm-growing conditions. The plants need constant misting as they do not tolerate drying out for extended periods. This orchid dislikes disturbance, and healthy plants are best left alone.

🌡 *Cool* ✵ *Shade*

Acacallis cyanea is a striking species with "blue" flowers (really a pink flushed lilac-mauve).

AMESIELLA

(after Oakes Ames, an American orchidologist) (pronounced: aim-SEE-el-ah)

An attractive monopodial genus from the Philippines, consisting of three species. The orchids have short spikes bearing up to five disproportionately large crystalline white flowers which bloom in winter and spring.

🌡 *Intermediate* ✵ *Semi-shade*

Amesiella monticola is a robust species that has shapely, large pure-white flowers with a three-lobed labellum and a long spur. This spur is filled with nectar which is fragrant at night and attracts moths. This species comes from the mountains of central Luzon in the Philippines. It prefers cool to intermediate conditions and grows well in *Sphagnum* moss or on cork slabs if watered frequently.

ANCISTROCHILUS

(from the Greek, ankistron = hook, and cheilos = lip, referring to the shape of the labellum)
(pronounced: an-sis-tro-KIE-lus)

The two species within this African genus have only recently entered cultivation. They enjoy warm conditions. Adult plants must be given a dry rest in winter, but do not allow the pseudobulbs to shrivel. They enjoy bright light, but not excessive levels which will scorch the thin leaves. Water them generously when in active growth. Small plants do well in moss, while adult plants can be grown in a free-draining bark-based mix. Larger specimens can be established onto horizontal cork rafts. Both species bloom during the warmer months.

🌡 *Warm* ☀ *Bright*

Catasetum Orchidglade is a primary hybrid between C. expansum and C. pileatum. C. expansum is from Ecuador. It has showy blooms that are cream to golden yellow, often with maroon spotting on the petals and its flat labellum. C. pileatum is one of the most popular species in cultivation, bearing up to twelve, 4-inch (100-mm) blooms, that range in color from pure white to green-yellow, with no spotting.

🌡 *Intermediate* ☀ *Bright*

Ancistrochilus rothschildianus is from tropical western Africa. It produces small upright sprays of two or three pink to mauve blooms, up to 3 inches (75 mm) across. *A. thomsonianus* is the closely related species.

CATASETUM

(from the Greek, kata = downward, and Latin, seta = bristle, referring to the position of the two horns on the column) (pronounced: KAT-ah-see-tum)

A genus of 70 robust epiphytes from Central and South America, with fleshy pseudobulbs and up to eight short-lived leaves. Plants produce inflorescences bearing either male or female flowers. The plants generate colorful and attractive male flowers in ideal conditions, with the fleshy and somewhat bland female blooms being produced when the plant is under stress. The male blooms display a most unusual and very fast pollen-ejection mechanism. Catasetums enjoy intermediate to warm conditions and require copious water and fertilizer when in full growth to maximize the size of the pseudobulbs. The plants should be watered sparingly after the pseudobulbs have shed their leaves in winter. These naked bulbs often have sharp spines where the leaves were attached, so care must be taken when handling the plants.

COELIA

(from the Greek, koilos = hollow, the pseudobulbs were mistakenly thought to be hollow, like some Schomburgkia species) (pronounced: so-EEL-ee-ah)

This is a Central American genus with five species, even though some authorities include most members within *Bothriochilus*. They are sympodial and terrestrials, distantly related to *Calanthe* and *Phaius*, and have round pseudobulbs topped with a few plicate leaves. These do best in intermediate conditions and require a lot of water and fertilizer during the spring growing season, to plump up the pseudobulbs. They need to be kept dry during their winter dormancy. Most species bloom with the new growths in spring.

Coelia bella is without doubt the most spectacular and eye-catching member of the genus with its pink-tipped, white, 2-inch (50-mm), fragrant flowers with a bright yellow labellum. It is a spring-flowerer, native to Mexico and Guatemala and can have up to eight blooms on an upright inflorescence.

🌡 *Intermediate* ✺ *Semi-shade* ✿ *Perfumed*

CUITLAUZINA

(after King Cuitlahuatzin of Mexico) (pronounced: kweet-law-ZEE-nah)

This is a monotypic genus (only one representative) from Mexico. It is best grown in a pot or basket because of its pendulous flowering habit. It needs a cool dry rest in winter, when it should be watered just enough to keep the pseudobulbs from shriveling. The flower spikes often emerge when the new growth is barely 1 inch (25 mm) long, and is very brittle at this stage. The blooms are susceptible to *Botrytis* fungal attack if left in a humid area without plenty of air circulation.

🌡 *Cool* ✺ *Semi-shade* ✿ *Perfumed*

Cuitlauzina pendula was previously well known as *Odontoglossum pendulum* or *O. citrosmum*. It produces pendent sprays (which rarely branch) with the immature new growth, which can have up to 20 waxy, long-lived blooms with a faint but distinct lemon scent. The 3-inch (75-mm) flowers have white to pink petals and sepals with a darker pink to purple labellum. It is a beautiful species that never fails to impress when seen in full bloom.

DYAKIA

(after the native Dyak people of Borneo)
(pronounced: di-ACK-ee-ah)

A monotypic genus from
Borneo, previously included
within the genus *Ascocentrum*.
It differs from that genus by its
floral structure as well as its
flat leaves (they are strongly
channeled in *Ascocentrum*). These
orchids are compact and require
warm to hot, moist conditions
throughout the year, and grow
best in either small pots or cork
mounts.

🌡 *Warm* ☀ *Bright*

Dyakia hendersonianum has
upright spikes of vivid rose to
magenta flowers with a contrasting
white labellum.

EMBREEA

(after Alvin Embree, a South American orchidologist) (pronounced: em-BREE-ah)

There are two species within this genus from Colombia and Ecuador,
which are closely related to *Stanhopea*. They have four-angled
pseudobulbs topped with a single leaf that has a grayish-green tinge.
Embreea prefer intermediate to warm conditions in a moist atmosphere
and the plants will not stand bright sunlight. Basket culture is
recommended due to the pendulous inflorescences and they need to be
grown in a medium that is moisture-retentive. Like *Stanhopeas*, the
flowers last only a few days.

🌡 *Intermediate* ☀ *Shade* ✽ *Perfumed*

Embreea rodigasiana has very large
individual blooms, which are up to
6 inches (150 mm) across. A mature
plant will have many flowers. It is an
unforgettable sight. This is closely
related to the genus *Stanhopea*.

EUCHILE

(from the Greek euchile = beautiful lip, referring to the prominent labellum of both species)
(pronounced: you-KY-lee)

The generic name Euchile was proposed in 1998; previously it was treated as a section within the broad genus *Encyclia. Euchile citrina,* and its sister species *E. mariae,* are both endemic to Mexico and are the only members of their genus. They have pseudobulbs covered in whitish scales, and glaucous leaves. They must have a cool dry rest in winter, and will take high temperatures in summer, provided the humidity is also high and the plants are shaded from direct sunlight. Grow the plants on generous slabs of virgin cork, with the plants tied on (facing downward) to slabs hanging vertically.

❄ *Cool* ☼ *Bright* ❀ *Perfumed*

Euchile citrina is a spectacular pendent-growing species. With its bright yellow glossy blooms, it has been called the "daffodil" or "tulip orchid." The flowers have a strong pleasant citrus fragrance, hence the name *citrina.* Usually only one flower is produced, yet strong plants can carry twin blooms. This species is dormant during the cooler months, during which time the plants should not be watered.

LEPTOTES

(from the Greek, leptotes = delicacy, referring to their delicate appearance) (pronounced: lep-TOTE-eez)

This is a small genus of about five distinctive epiphytes. These terete-leafed plants do equally well in pots of a coarse mixture, on treefern or cork slabs, or in small wooden baskets. They like bright light and intermediate conditions, even though they are quite adaptable to a wide temperature range.

❄ *Intermediate* ☼ *Bright*

Leptotes bicolor has 2-inch (50-mm) blooms, with white sepals and a purple labellum. The amount of purple varies. It has fleshy, terete leaves, up to 5 inches (120 mm) long. This reliable spring bloomer is native to Brazil.

MEDIOCALCAR

(from the Latin, medio = middle, and calcar = spur, referring to the spur that is attached at the middle of the labellum) (pronounced: mead-ee-oh-KAL-car)

This is a small group of creeping and scrambling orchids that come from the highlands of New Guinea and the Pacific Islands. They have varying growth habits, but very similar, globular, glossy blooms that appear from the immature new growth, either singly or in pairs. They have been called "cherry orchids," because their unique blooms resemble the fruit. Small species perform well in shallow pots of *Sphagnum* moss, while larger plants can be grown on treefern rafts, as long as the substrate is kept moist. They detest hot, dry conditions and must be kept moist in a buoyant atmosphere. Most species bloom from fall to early spring.

Mediocalcar decoratum has petite pseudobulbs, topped with three or four small, but succulent, green to purple-stained leaves and has bright orange blooms with yellow tips to the segments. It blooms in the fall and winter.

🌡 *Cool* ❊ *Shade*

STANHOPEA

(after the British Earl of Stanhope) (pronounced: stan-HOPE-ee-ah)

This is a large and popular genus, known from Mexico to Brazil. The plants are grown for their large, bizarre, colorful blooms. Even though the highly fragrant flowers last for only a few days, they have much to offer the plant enthusiast. The labellum structure alone is simply amazing. Stanhopeas need to be grown in baskets, to allow their pendent spikes to penetrate through the medium and burst into bloom. They are not particularly fussy about the growing medium; with *Sphagnum* moss, *Cymbidium* compost or fine grade, pine bark being used either exclusively or in combination with other materials. They appreciate constant moisture throughout the year, and grow best in a semi-shaded position. The leaves will readily burn if given very strong light, combined with low humidity. Being such a varied genus, there are species suitable for cool to tropical climates, with the promise of blooms over several months.

🌡 *Cool* ❊ *Semi-shade* ❀ *Perfumed*

Stanhopea nigroviolacea is a Mexican, summer flowering species, with pairs of yellow-green blooms, which are heavily blotched with dark red-brown. It has a pleasant but powerful vanilla fragrance that is often detected before sighting the blooms. *S. tigrina* is a closely related species with paler blooms.

🌡 *Intermediate* ❊ *Semi-shade* ❀ *Perfumed*

Stanhopea oculata is an elegant, variable species, which is found from Mexico to Brazil. It has up to eight flowers, which are pale yellow, overlaid with red purple spots that can look like circles. The labellum is cream, with some fine, reddish, pepper spotting and is bright orange at the base.

MISCELLANEOUS TERRESTRIAL GENERA

ARUNDINA
(from the Latin, arundo = reed, referring to its reed-like stems) (pronounced: ar-run-DEEN-ah)

Arundina is a genus of some eight species with a wide distribution from northern India across Asia to the Pacific Islands. All the species are terrestrials suitable for gardens in warm zones. If grown in a glasshouse, select a large pot to accommodate the extensive root system. Plants can be propagated from aerial growths that are produced along the upper nodes of the bamboo-like pseudobulbs. The flowers last only a day or two, but are produced in such numbers that large plants are always in bloom. *Arundina graminifolia* has become a weed in Hawaii, colonizing old lava flows to the extent that many consider this to be an indigenous plant.

Arundina graminifolia is a widespread species with attractive flowers that resemble a small *Cattleya*. They range in color from white to the deepest purple, often with contrasting shades on the labellum.

Warm ❂ *Bright*

BONETEA
(after Giuseppe Antonio Bonat, an Italian botanist) (pronounced: bon-ET-ee-ah)

Bonatea is a genus of 20 species found throughout southern and eastern Africa. It is related to the pan-tropical genus *Habenaria*. The orchids require moist and cool to intermediate conditions when in growth, from fall to spring. They are best grown in deep pots with a well-drained terrestrial mix, containing a high proportion of peat moss and coarse sand. They will be dormant in summer, at which time they should be kept dry until growth restarts in the fall.

Cool ❂ *Semi-shade*

Bonatea speciosa is one of the most impressive species in the genus. It is from southeastern Africa and can produce tall inflorescences up to 40 inches (1 m) tall, carrying numerous, densely packed green and white blooms in spring.

CYPRIPEDIUM

(from the Greek Cypros, the sacred island to Venus, and pedilon = slipper)
(pronounced: sip-re-PEE-dee-um)

The deciduous genus *Cypripedium* consists of 50 species that are found in North and Central America, Europe, and Asia. They are one of the most impressive terrestrial genera, and well known as "Lady's Slipper Orchids." In cool to temperate climates, these herbaceous perennials can be grown in pots or in the garden in soils rich in decayed leaf matter. They do not grow in subtropical or tropical climates.

Cypripedium kentuckiense is from Kentucky, USA. It has large flowers up to 6 inches (150 mm) across that vary in color from white to pale cream and amber. It is one of the easier species to cultivate in deep pots.

 *Cool* *Semi-shade*

 *Cool* *Semi-shade*

Cypripedium formosanum is restricted to the high mountains of Taiwan. It has a pair of attractive fan-like wavy leaves and a single pink flower that is up to 3½ inches (90 mm) across. This species will grow only in cool conditions—it detests heat.

DISA

(after the mythical Queen Disa of Sweden) (pronounced: DYE-sa)

This is primarily a South African genus, and the famous *Disa uniflora* is known as "The Pride of Table Mountain." In the wild, disas are found growing on the fringes of marshlands, or the banks of flowing streams, so it is no surprise that *Sphagnum* moss is the best medium for cultivated plants. They are very particular about water quality and rainwater is preferable. The plants should be kept moist throughout the year. Do not sit the plants in trays of water for extended periods, otherwise you run the risk of rotting the tubers. Mature plants may produce daughter plants at the edge of the pot (or frustratingly at times through the drainage holes!) These can be potted separately when large enough to handle. Disas should be repotted each fall into fresh moss, after the main summer flowering period. They enjoy cool to intermediate conditions. There are numerous attractive hybrids, many with a high percentage of *Disa uniflora* in their pedigree. The color range is also expanding with whites, lemons, and pinks now supplementing the reds and oranges.

❄ *Cool* ✪ *Semi-shade*

Disa Kewensis is a primary hybrid, registered in 1893, between *Disa uniflora* and the smaller flowered species *D. tripetaloides*, which has white to pink blooms with darker spotting.

Disa uniflora *(left)* is the most magnificent plant species from South Africa. Despite its name, this species can produce up to six flowers on an erect inflorescence, during summer. The large (up to 6 inches [150 mm]) flowers vary in color from a brilliant scarlet-red through various shades of orange. There are some rare, yellow (or lutea) forms.

❄ *Cool* ✪ *Semi-shade*

Disa Kewbett 'Pure' *(right)* has almost 70 percent *Disa uniflora* in its breeding, mostly using the rare yellow flowered form.

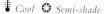

❄ *Cool* ✪ *Semi-shade*

❄ *Cool* ✪ *Semi-shade*

Disa Watsonii is a hybrid originally registered in 1900, between *Disa uniflora* and *Disa Kewensis (right).*

PTEROSTYLIS

(from the Greek pteron = wing, and stylos = style, referring to the wings on the column of the flower) (pronounced: terr-oh-STY-lis)

This is a large genus of over 160 temperate, deciduous terrestrials, known as "greenhoods," with the majority of the species occurring in Australia. There are also representatives from New Zealand, New Caledonia, and New Guinea. Most species have green blooms with red-brown suffusions and transparent "light windows" to deceive pollinators that would normally avoid a restricted, darker area. The labellum is sensitive, mobile, and capable of rapid movement. This acts as an important attractant for potential pollinators. Most species have a rosette of leaves, with the single bloom produced on a slender stem, originating from the crown of the foliage. They require moist, humid, and cool conditions when in growth during the fall to spring. *Pterostylis* are best grown in a well-drained terrestrial mix, containing a high proportion of peat moss and coarse sand. They are dormant in summer when they revert to round, white tubers that are about ½ inch (12 mm) in diameter, and should be kept dry during this period. They are best repotted annually, repositioning the dormant tubers 2 inches (50 mm) below the soil surface. The following two species are "rosette" types, from southeastern Australia.

🌡 *Cool* ✲ *Shade*

Pterostylis baptistii is the largest flowered of the Australian species. It has large, bulbous green and white flowers, on tall stems, in spring. Keep this species moist for another two months after flowering, to ensure prolific stolon and tuber production. The awarded clone 'Greenpoint' is particularly vigorous.

🌡 *Cool* ✲ *Shade*

Pterostylis curta is also from eastern Australia and has dark green and white flowers, with a light brown labellum that has a distinctive slight twist. It blooms in early spring. Being a very hardy species makes this an ideal choice for beginners. There is also a variegated leafed form.

SOBRALIA

(after Francisco Sobral, Spanish botanist) (pronounced: so-BRAL-ee-ah)

Sobralia comprises 100 species of leafy, terrestrial orchids from tropical Central and South America. The very large *Cattleya*-like species have blooms that grow from the top of the cane-like stalks. These bloom in the summer and are often short-lived. They need to be potted into large, deep containers, to accommodate the extensive, thick root system. A well-drained terrestrial mix, with the addition of bark is ideal. Intermediate to warm conditions suit most species. The plants enjoy strong light, coupled with frequent watering and feeding during the warm months. Keep the plants on the dry side during the winter, when the growth rate is significantly reduced.

🌡 *Intermediate* ✲ *Bright*

Sobralia macrantha has stems that can grow up to 7 feet (2 m) tall, but are less in cultivation. This Central American species has very large rose-purple to pure white flowers that are up to 10 inches (250 mm) across.

Sobralia xantholeuca is from Central America, with a similar habit to *S. macrantha*. It has slightly nodding lemon yellow flowers that are up to 8 inches (200 mm) across.

Intermediate ✸ *Bright*

THUNIA
(after Franz von Thun, Bohemian orchid enthusiast) (pronounced: THOO-nee-ah)

This is a small group of terrestrial orchids, from Nepal to Indochina. They have upright, thick, cane-like pseudobulbs, with numerous, short-lived, thin leaves. Thunias are summer blooming plants, producing clusters of large, *Cattleya*-like blooms that are slightly nodding, with white, persistent floral bracts. The labellum is colorful, bell-shaped, and showy, covered with fine hairs. They are dormant and completely leafless through winter. Repotting is best undertaken at this time, into deep pots of a rich well-drained terrestrial mix. New shoots start growing in early spring, and develop quickly over the next few months. During the growing phase, plants need very strong light, and should be placed in a tray of water, up to 2 inches (50 mm) deep. Slow release fertilizers may also be applied during this time, as they are heavy feeders during their period of rapid growth. In the fall, allow the plants to dry out—the leaves will yellow, wither, and fall over, leaving them naked for winter, when they must be kept cool and dry.

Cool ✸ *Bright*

Thunia Veitchiana 'Jannine' is frequently mistaken for a species, but is a primary hybrid between the scarce *Thunia bensoniae* and *T. marshalliana*. It has white segments with a pink flush, and a bright purple labellum with a few orange markings.

APPENDIX

Season	Checklist of Jobs

SPRING

- *Provide as much light as you can to your plants, without scorching their leaves.*

- *Most genera are starting their growth phase. This is the best time of year to repot and divide most orchid plants.*

- *Provide plenty of water to your plants—making sure the water is freely flowing out of the drainage holes. Usually twice to three times a week should be enough.*

- *Liquid fertilizer to be applied to plants every second watering, as most are in active growth. Some granules of a three-month slow release fertilizer may also be applied either on or just under the surface of the potting medium.*

SUMMER

- *Ensure your orchids have adequate shading, avoid direct light on shade loving plants.*

- *Keep humidity levels high during times of extreme heat. Mist the foliage frequently.*

- *Provide plenty of water to your plants—making sure the water is freely flowing out of the drainage holes. During warm spells, this should be every second day.*

- *Liquid fertilizer to be applied to plants in active growth, every third watering.*

Season	Checklist of Jobs
FALL/AUTUMN	• *Be cautious of heat waves at the beginning of the season as well as early frosty conditions toward the end.* • *Stake up new growths on your plants to keep them upright.* • *The frequency of watering needs to be reduced to once every five to seven days. Most orchids with pseudobulbs will have completed their new growths.* • *Reduce fertilizer, only applying once every three weeks.*
WINTER	• *Ensure your orchids are not subjected to frost or freezing conditions.* • *Many types are in a dormant phase, so do a thorough check for pests such as scale and mealy bugs that also prefer dryer conditions. Remove any dead leaves and spent flowering stems.* • *Plants have reduced moisture requirements in winter, and generally only require watering every seven to ten days. Orchid genera that become deciduous and fully dormant only need a quick watering every three weeks, enough to keep the pseudobulbs plump.* • *Fertilizer should not be applied to plants in dormant state.* • *Now is the time to take stock of your orchid accessories, ensure you have enough pots, bark, plastic tags, potting medium, fertilizer, etc, for the months ahead.*

GLOSSARY

AERIAL a young plant, that develops older pseudobulbs or inflorescences, also known as keikis.

AERIAL ROOTS erect adventitious roots which often collect leaf litter.

ANGRAECOID an orchid genus related to *ANGRAECUM.*

ANTHER the pollen-bearing part of the stamen.

AXIS the point between the leaf and the main stem.

BACK-BULB older (and often leafless) pseudobulbs that may re-shoot if severed from the main plant.

BIFOLIATE with two leaves.

BOTANICALS small growing and miniature flowered species of limited horticultural interest.

BRACT a leaf-like structure.

BUD an unopened flower or a new shoot in its early stages.

BULBILS small bulb-like structures from which new plants can develop.

CAPSULE a fruit containing many seeds.

CLEISTOGAMOUS flowers that self-pollinate without opening.

CLONE a group of genetically identical plants, propagated vegetatively from one individual.

COLUMN the central, fleshy part of the orchid flower comprising the sexual organs.

COMPLEX HYBRID a hybrid involving more than two different species.

CULTIVAR a selected, and often superior, horticultural variety of a species or hybrid.

DECIDUOUS the seasonal shedding of leaves, which live for less than a year.

DORMANT resting, not in active growth.

ENDEMIC restricted to a particular country, region or area.

EPHEMERAL short-lived.

EPIPHYTE/EPIPHYTIC a plant that grows on trees, but is not parasitic.

EVERGREEN retaining leaves throughout the year.

EXOTIC from overseas.

EYE small dormant growth from which flowers or leaves may develop.

FIMBRIATED of a margin fringed with fine hairs or threads.

FLORA pertaining to plants.

FLORIFEROUS to produce many flowers.

GENERA plural of genus.

GENUS a group of related species, a taxonomic category above species.

GREX a specific hybrid combination.

GROWTH vegetative shoot.

HYBRID the progeny of a cross between two different species or other hybrids.

INDIGENOUS native to a country, region or area.

INFLORESCENCE the flowering stem of a plant.

KEIKI Hawaiian term for aerial growths.

LABELLUM a modified petal, also known as the lip.

LITHOPHYTE a plant that grows on rocks.

MERICLONE a plant derived vegetatively from tissue culture that is genetically identical to its parent.

MINIATURE little, small, pertaining to plant habit and/or flowers.

MONOPODIAL having one main or primary stem, producing leaves and flowers along that stem.

MONTANE from the mountains.

MONOTYPIC a genus with a single species.

MYCORRHIZAL a type of fungus.

NATURAL HYBRID a rare naturally occurring hybrid between two different species.

NOMENCLATURE the rules governing valid names.

OVARY the structure directly behind the flower that develops into the fruit or capsule.

PEDUNCLE the part of the flowering stem before the first flower starts.

PENDENT hanging downward.

PERLITE a synthetic growing medium.

PHOTOSYNTHESIZE the process of growth by which plants convert sunlight into usable growth food for the plant.

POLLINIA a group of pollen grains massed together.

PRIMARY HYBRID the initial hybrid between two different species.

PROTOCORM a germinating orchid seed.

PSEUDOBULB the thickened or bulb-like stem of a sympodial orchid.

RHIZOME a specialized stem from which roots and shoots are produced along its length.

SAPROPHYTE a leafless, non-green plant that lives off decaying plant matter.

SECTION in a plant classification context, a group of closely related species.

SEEDLING a young plant raised from seed, that has yet to flower.

SHOOT a term used for a new growth.

SLAB a medium or mount for growing orchids on, such as cork and treefern.

SPECIES a taxonomic grouping of closely related individuals, with set characters, that differs from other species.

SPECIES ORCHID orchids as they naturally occur in the wild.

STAMEN the male part of a flower producing pollen.

STIGMA the sticky receptive part of the column, which accepts pollen.

SUBSPECIES taxonomic rank below species, often used to describe distinct geographical populations.

SYMPODIAL a growth habit whereby each stem has limited growth and new shoots develop from the base of previous ones.

SYNONYM a previous invalid name for a species.

TAXA plural of taxon.

TAXON a term used to describe a taxonomic group, for example genus, species.

TAXONOMY the classification of plants and animals.

TERETE slender, cylindrical, and round in cross-sec.

TERRESTRIAL a plant that grows in or on the ground.

TUBER a thickened, underground storage organ.

TYPE the original representative of a species, genus or other taxon.

UNIFOLIATE with one leaf.

VANDACEOUS a collective group of monopodial orchids related to *VANDA*.

VARIETY taxonomic rank below species, often used for minor differences or color forms.

SELECTED BIBLIOGRAPHY

Ames, O. & D.S. Correll (1985). *Orchids of Guatemala and Belize.* Dover Publications, New York.

Banks, D.P. (1999). *Tropical Orchids of Southeast Asia.* Periplus Editions, Hong Kong.

Barretto, G.D. & J.L. Young Saye (1980). *Hong Kong Orchids.* Urban Council, Hong Kong.

Bechtel H., P. Cribb & E. Launert (1992). *The Manual of Cultivated Orchid Species* (third edition). Blandford, London.

Bishop, T. (2000). *Field Guide to the Orchids of New South Wales and Victoria* (second edition). UNSW Press, Sydney.

Bockemühl, L. (1989). *Odontoglossum. A monograph and iconograph.* Brücke-Verlag Kurt Schmersow, Hildesheim

Bose, T.K. & S.K. Bhattacharjee (1980). *Orchids of India.* Naya Prokash, Calcutta.

Braem, G.J., C.O. Baker & M.L. Baker (1998). *The Genus Paphiopedilum, Natural History and Cultivation.* Volume 1. Botanical Publishers, Florida.

Braem, G.J., C.O. Baker & M.L. Baker (1999). *The Genus Paphiopedilum, Natural History and Cultivation.* Volume 2. Botanical Publishers, Florida.

Chan, C.L., A. Lamb, P.S. Shim & J.J. Wood (1994). *Orchids of Borneo.* Vol. 1. Introduction and a selection of species. Royal Botanic Gardens, Kew.

Christenson, E.A. (2001). *Phalaenopsis, A Monograph.* Timber Press, Portland.

Clayton, D. (2002). *The Genus Coelogyne, A Synopsis.* Natural History Publications, Kota Kinabula, Borneo.

Clements, M.A. & D.L. Jones (1996). New Species of Dendrobiinae (Orchidaceae) from Papua New Guinea. *Lasianthera* 1:(1) 8-25.

Clements, M.A. & D.L. Jones (1997). A Preliminary Taxonomic Review of *Grastidium* Blume and *Eriopexis* (Schltr.) Brieger (Orchidaceae). *Lasianthera* 1: (2) 52-128.

Clements, M.A. (1989). Catalogue of Australian Orchidaceae. *Australian Orchid Research.* Volume 1. Australian Orchid Foundation. Melbourne.

Comber, J.B. (1990). *Orchids of Java.* Royal Botanic Gardens, Kew.

Cootes, J. (2001). *The Orchids of the Philippines.* Times Editions, Singapore.

Cribb, P. & C. Bailes (1989). *Hardy Orchids.* Timber Press, Portland.

Cribb, P. & I. Butterfield (1989). *The Genus Pleione.* Timber Press, Portland.

Cribb, P. & W.A. Whistler (1996). *Orchids of Samoa.* Royal Botanic Gardens, Kew.

Cribb, P. (1998). *The Genus Paphiopedilum* (second edition) Natural History Publications, Kota Kinabalu.

Cullen, J. {ed.} (1992). *The Orchid Book. A guide to the identification of cultivated orchid species.* Cambridge University Press, New York.

de Vogel, E.F. (1988). Revisions of Coelogyninae (Orchidaceae) III. The Genus *Pholidota. Orchid Monographs* 3: 1-116. Leiden.

Dockrill, A.W. (1992). *Australian Indigenous Orchids.* Volumes 1 & 2. (revised edition). Surrey Beatty & Sons, Sydney.

Dodson, C.H. & R. Escobar (1994). *Native Ecuadorian Orchids.* Vol. 1. *Aa – Dracula* Editorial Colina, Medellin.

Dressler, R.L. (1981). *The Orchids. Natural History and Classification.* Harvard University Press, Cambridge.

Dressler, R.L. (1993). *Field Guide to the Orchids of Coast Rica and Panama.* Cornell University Press, New York.

Dressler, R.L. & G.E. Pollard (1976). *The Genus Encyclia in Mexico.* Asociación Mexicana de Orquideología, Mexico.

Du Puy, D. & P. Cribb (1988). *The Genus Cymbidium.* Timber Press, Portland.

Du Puy, D., P. Cribb, J. Bosser, J. Hermans & C. Hermans (1999). *The Orchids of Madagascar.* Royal Botanic Gardens, Kew.

Dunsterville, G.C.K. & L.A. Garay (1959). *Venezuelan Orchids Illustrated.* Vol. I. Harvard University, Cambridge.

Dunsterville, G.C.K. & L.A. Garay (1961). *Venezuelan Orchids Illustrated.* Vol. II. Harvard University, Cambridge.

Dunsterville, G.C.K. & L.A. Garay (1965). *Venezuelan Orchids Illustrated.* Vol. III. Harvard University, Cambridge.

Dunsterville, G.C.K. & L.A. Garay (1966). *Venezuelan Orchids Illustrated.* Vol. IV. Harvard University, Cambridge.

Dunsterville, G.C.K. & L.A. Garay (1972). *Venezuelan Orchids Illustrated.* Vol. V. Harvard University, Cambridge.

Dunsterville, G.C.K. & L.A. Garay (1976). *Venezuelan Orchids Illustrated.* Vol. VI. Harvard University, Cambridge.

LEFT *A purple and red Odontoglossum, photographed at McBean's Orchid Nursery in East Sussex, England.*

Escobar, R {ed.} (1990). *Native Colombian Orchids.* Vol. 1. *Acacallis – Dryadella.* Editorial Colina, Medellin.

Escobar, R {ed.} (1991). *Native Colombian Orchids.* Vol. 2. *Elleanthus Masdevallia.* Editorial Colina, Medellin.

Escobar, R {ed.} (1991). *Native Colombian Orchids.* Vol. 3. *Maxillaria – Ponthieva.* Editorial Colina, Medellin.

Escobar, R {ed.} (1992). *Native Colombian Orchids.* Vol. 4. *Porroglossum – Zygosepalum.* Editorial Colina, Medellin.

Escobar, R {ed.} (1994). *Native Colombian Orchids.* Vol. 5. Supplement, *Aa – Lepanthes.* Editorial Colina, Medellin.

Escobar, R {ed.} (1998). *Native Colombian Orchids.* Vol. 6. Supplement, *Leucohyle – Zootrophion.* Editorial Colina, Medellin.

Fessel, H.H. & P. Balzer (1999). *A Selection of Native Philippine Orchids.* Times Editions, Singapore.

Fowlie, J.A. (1977). *The Brazilian Bifoliate Cattleyas and Their Color Varieties.* Azul Quinta Press, Pomona.

Garay, L.A., F. Hamer & E.S. Siegerist (1994). The genus *Cirrhopetalum* and the genera of the *Bulbophyllum* alliance. *Nordic Journal of Botany* 14: 609-646. Copenhagen.

Gibbs, A., A. Mackenzie, A. Blanchfield, P. Cross, C. Wilson, E. Kitojima, M. Nightingale & M. Clements (2000). Viruses of orchids in Australia; their identification, biology and control. *Australian Orchid Review* 65: (3) 10-21.

Golamco, A. (1991). *Philippines' Book on Orchids.* Jemma, Rizal.

Greer, B. (1998). *The Astonishing Stanhopeas.* Graphic World, Sydney.

Grove, D.L. (1995). *Vandas and Ascocendas and Their Combinations with Other Genera.* Timber Press, Portland.

Hawkes, A.D. (1965). *Encyclopaedia of Cultivated Orchids.* (1987 reprint) Faber and Faber, London.

Hillerman, F.E. & A.W. Holst (1986). *An Introduction to the Cultivated Angraecoid Orchids of Madagascar.* Timber Press, Portland.

Holst, A.W. (1999). *The World of Catasetums.* Timber Press, Portland.

Isaac-Williams, M.L. (1988). *An Introduction to the Orchids of Asia.* Angus & Robertson, Sydney.

Jenny, R. (1993). *Monograph of the Genus Gongora.* Koeltz, Illinois.

Johns, J. & B. Molloy (1983). *Native Orchids of New Zealand.* Reed, Wellington.

Jones, D.L. (1988). *Native Orchids of Australia.* Reed, Sydney.

La Croix, I. & E. La Croix (1997). *African Orchids in the Wild and in Cultivation.* Timber Press, Portland.

Lavarack, P.S., W. Harris & G. Stocker (2000). *Dendrobium and its Relatives.* Kangaroo Press, Sydney.

Lewis, B.A. & P.J. Cribb (1991). *Orchids of the Solomon Islands and Bougainville.* Royal Botanic Gardens, Kew.

Luer, C.A. (1986). Systematics of the Pleurothallidinae (Orchidaceae). *Icones Pleurothallidinarum* I: 1-81. Missouri Botanical Garden, Sarasota.

Luer, C.A. (1986). Systematics of *Masdevallia* (Orchidaceae). *Icones Pleurothallidinarum* II 1-63. Missouri Botanical Garden, Sarasota.

Luer, C.A. (1986). Systematics of *Pleurothallis* (Orchidaceae). *Icones Pleurothallidinarum* III: 1-109. Missouri Botanical Garden, Sarasota.

Luer, C.A. (1993). Systematics of *Dracula. Icones Pleurothallidinarum* X: 1-244. Missouri Botanical Garden, Sarasota.

Luer, C.A. (1996). Systematics of *Restrepia* (Orchidaceae). *Icones Pleurothallidinarum* XIII: 1-168. Missouri Botanical Garden, Sarasota.

McLeish, I., N.R. Pearce & B.R. Adams (1995). *Native Orchids of Belize.* A.A. Balkema Publishers, Rotterdam.

McQueen, J. & B. McQueen (1993). *Orchids of Brazil.* Text Publishing Co., Melbourne.

Mayr, H. & M. Schmucker (1998). *Orchid Names and their Meanings.* Gantner Verlag, Vaduz.

Millar, A. (1999). *Orchids of Papua New Guinea.* Crawford House Publishing, Bathurst.

Miller, D. & R. Warren (1994). *Orchids of the High Mountain Atlantic Rainforest in Southeastern Brazil.* Salamandra Consultoria, Rio de Janeiro.

Motes, M.R. (1997). *Vandas. Their Botany, History, and Culture.* Timber Press, Portland.

Mulder, D. & T. Mulder-Roelfsema (1990). *Orchids Travel by Air.* Het Houten Hert, Netherlands.

Neal, J. (1994). *Growing Phalaenopsis at Home.* Earth Productions, Sydney.

Northen, R.T. (1990). *Home Orchid Growing* (fourth edition). Prentice Hall Press, New York.

Northen, R.T. (1996). *Miniature Orchids and How to Grow Them.* Dover Publications, New York.

O'Byrne, P. (1994). *Lowland Orchids of Papua New Guinea.* SNP Publishers, Singapore.

Oakeley, H (1993). *Lycaste Species. The Essential Guide.* Vigo Press, London.

Oakeley, H (2000). *Anguloa – a history. Australian Orchid Review* 65:(5) 4-10.

Pedersen, H.Æ. (1997). The genus *Dendrochilum* (Orchidaceae) in the Philippines – a taxonomic revision. *Opera Botanica* 131: 1-205. Copenhagen.

Pedersen, H.Æ., J.J. Wood & J.B. Comber (1997). A revised subdivision and biblio- graphical survey of *Dendrochilum* (Orchidaceae). *Opera Botanica* 130: 1-85. Copenhagen.

Pradhan, U.C. & S.C. Pradhan (1997). *100 Beautiful Himalayan Orchids and How to Grow Them.* Primulaceae Books, West Bengal.

Pridgeon, A. {ed.} (1992). *What Orchid is That?* Weldon Publishing, Sydney.

Rhodehamel, W.A. (1991). *A Masdevallia Cultural Guide.* Rhodehamel, Indianapolis.

Riley, J.J. & D.P. Banks (2002). *Orchids of Australia.* UNSW Press, Kensington, Australia.

Schlechter, R. (1982). *The Orchidaceae of German New Guinea.* (English translation). Australian Orchid Foundation, Melbourne.

Schuiteman, A. (1997). Revision of the Genus *Mediocalcar* (Orchidaceae). *Orchid Monographs* 8: 21-77, 189-208 {line drawings}. Leiden.

Schultes, R.E. & A.S. Pease (1963). *Generic Names of Orchids. Their Origin and Meaning.* Academic Press, New York.

Seidenfaden, G. (1973). *Notes on Cirrhopetalum. Dansk Botanisk Arkiv.* 29(1)

Seidenfaden, G. (1979). *Orchid Genera in Thailand* VIII. *Bulbophyllum. Dansk Botanisk Arkiv.*33(3)

Seidenfaden, G. (1992). The Orchids of Indochina. *Opera Botanica* 114: 1-502. Copenhagen.

Seidenfaden, G. & T. Smitinand (1965). *The Orchids of Thailand.* The Siam Society, Bangkok.

Seidenfaden, G. & J.J. Wood (1992). *The Orchids of Peninsular Malaysia and Singapore.* Olsen & Olsen, Fredensborg.

Soon, T.E. (1980). *Orchids of Asia.* Times Books International, Singapore.

St George, I. (1999). *The Nature Guide to New Zealand Native Orchids.* Random House, Auckland.

Stearn, W.T. (1983). *Botanical Latin* (third edition). David & Charles, London.

Stewart, J. & B. Campbell (1996). *Orchids of Kenya.* Timber Press, Portland.

Stewart, J. & M. Griffiths (1995). *RHS Manual of Orchids.* Timber Press, Portland.

Stewart, J., H.P. Linder, E.A. Schelpe & A.V. Hall (1982). *Wild Orchids of Southern Africa.* Macmillan, Johannesburg.

Sweet, H.R. (1980). *The Genus Phalaenopsis.* Orchid Digest, Pomona.

Tomlinson, P.C. (1983). *Oncidiums. A Cultural Guide.* Wellington Orchid Society, New Zealand.

Upton, W.T. (1989). *Dendrobium Orchids of Australia.* Houghton Mifflin, Melbourne.

Upton, W.T. (1992). *Sarcochilus Orchids of Australia.* 'Double U' Orchids, West Gosford.

Vaddhanaphuti, N (1997). *A Field Guide to the Wild Orchids of Thailand.* Silkworm Books, Chiang Mai.

Valmayor, H (1984). *Orchidiana Philippiniana.* Eugenio Lopez Foundation, Manila.

Vermeulen, J.J. (1987). A Taxonomic Revision of the Continental African Bulbophyllinae. *Orchid Monographs* 2: 1-300. Leiden.

Vermeulen, J.J. (1991). *Orchids of Borneo.* Vol.2. *Bulbophyllum.* Royal Botanic Gardens, Kew.

White, K. & B. Sharma (2000). *Wild Orchids in Nepal.* White Lotus Press, Bangkok.

Wiard, L.A. (1987). *An Introduction to the Orchids of Mexico.* Cornell University Press, New York.

Williams, B.S. & H. Williams (1961). *The Orchid-Grower's Manual* (seventh edition, reprint). Hafner Publishing, New York.

Withner, C.L. (1988). *The Cattleyas and their Relatives.* Vol. 1. The Cattleyas. Timber Press, Portland.

Withner, C.L. (1990). *The Cattleyas and their Relatives.* Vol. 2. The Laelias. Timber Press, Portland.

Withner, C.L. (1993). *The Cattleyas and their Relatives.* Vol. 3. *Schomburgkia, Sophronitis* and other South American Genera. Timber Press, Portland.

Withner, C.L. (1996). *The Cattleyas and their Relatives.* Vol. 4. The Bahamian and Caribbean Species. Timber Press, Portland.

Withner, C.L. (1998). *The Cattleyas and their Relatives.* Vol. 5. *Brassavola, Encyclia* and other Genera of Mexico and Central America. Timber Press, Portland.

Wodrich, K.H.K. (1997). *Growing South African Indigenous Orchids.* A.A. Balkema Publishers, Rotterdam.

Wood, J.J. & P.J. Cribb (1994). *A Checklist of the Orchids of Borneo.* Royal Botanic Gardens, Kew.

Wood, J.J. (1997). *Orchids of Borneo.* Vol. 3. *Dendrobium, Dendrochilum* and others. Royal Botanic Gardens, Kew.

220

INDEX

PICTURE CREDITS

KEY:- r = *right* l = *left* t = *top* b = *bottom* c = *center*

DAVID BANKS

10-br; 11; 13; 14-br; 17; 19; 20-tr; 24; 27-tl; 28-tr; 30-r; 34–39; 41; 43-r; 44-b; 49; 50; 52; 63 (all); 64-t; 67-br; 68-b; 77; 81; 82-b; 86-l & r; 88-l & r; 89; 90 (all); 91 (all); 92-tr; 93-r; 94-l & tr; 95-tl; 96 (all); 97-r; 98-b; 99-tl & tr; 100-r; 101; 102 (all); 103-tr; 104; 105; 106-tr & br; 107-l; 108; 109; 110 (all); 111-bl & tr; 112-tl, bl & br; 113-bl, tr, br; 114 (all); 115 (all); 116-tl, br; 117 (all); 118 (all); 119-br; 120-bl, tr, br; 121 (all); 122 (all); 123-tl, c, tr, br; 124 (all); 125-br; 126-tl, br; 127-bl, r; 128-tr, br; 131-tl & tr; 132; 133-l & tl; 134 (all); 135 (all); 136 (all); 137 (all); 138 (all); 139-tl & r; 141 (all); 142-c; 143; 145-l; 146-tr, br; 147 (all); 148-br; 149 (all); 150-br; 151-br; 152-bl & br; 153-bl & br; 154 (all); 155-tl, tr, br; 156 (all); 157 (all); 158 (all); 159; 160-bl; 161 (all); 162-l & tr; 163-t; 164; 165-tl, tr, bl; 166 (all); 170-tl & tr; 172-br; 173-tl & r; 174-bl & tr; 175-bl, tr, br; 176 (all); 177 (all); 178 (all); 179 (all); 180-t; 181 (all); 182 (all); 183 (all); 184 (all); 185 (all); 186-bl, bc, br; 187-tl & tr; 188-tl & bl; 189; 190-bl & br; 192 (all); 194-br; 195-tr & tl; 196-l; 197-r; 198 (all); 199 (all); 200 (all); 201 (all); 202 (all); 203 (all); 205 (all); 206-br; 207-l; 208-l; 209-r; 215.

GLOBAL

3; 12-b; 16 (all); 18; 20-tl; 29; 22; 23-b; 67-t; 85; 86-c; 87; 88-c; 92-l & b; 93-l; 94-br; 95-bl & r; 97-bl; 98-t; 99-b; 100-l; 103-tl & b; 106-l; 107-tr & br; 111-tl & br; 112-tr; 113-tl; 116-bl; 119-bl & tr; 120-tl; 123-br; 125-bl & tr; 126-bl & tr; 127-tl; 128-tl & bl; 129; 130 (all); 131-br; 133-br; 139-bl; 140 (all); 142-l & r; 144(all); 145-tr; 146-bl & bc; 148-tl & tr; 150-tl & tr; 151-tl & tr; 152-tl & tr; 153-tl; 155-bl; 160-tr; 162-br; 163-b; 165-br; 167 (all); 168 (all); 169 (all); 170-bl & br; 171 (all); 172-tr; 173-bl; 174-tl & br; 175-tl; 180-b; 186-tl, tr, rc; 187-b; 188-tl & bl; 190-tr; 191 (all); 193 (all); 194-l & tr; 195-b; 196-c & r; 197-l; 204 (all); 206-t; 207-c, tr, br; 208-c & br; 209-l.

SCIENCE PHOTO LIBRARY

14-bl; 15; 27-tr; 28-bl; 29; 30-l; 31–33; 45 (all); 48 (all).

THE ART ARCHIVE/ROYAL HORTICULTURAL SOCIETY/EILEEN TWEEDY

25 (all)

THE ORCHID REVIEW

23-t.